"Golf is deceptively simple and endlessly complicated; it satisfies the soul and frustrates the intellect, it is at the same time rewarding and maddening — and is without a doubt the greatest game mankind has ever invented"

Arnold Palmer

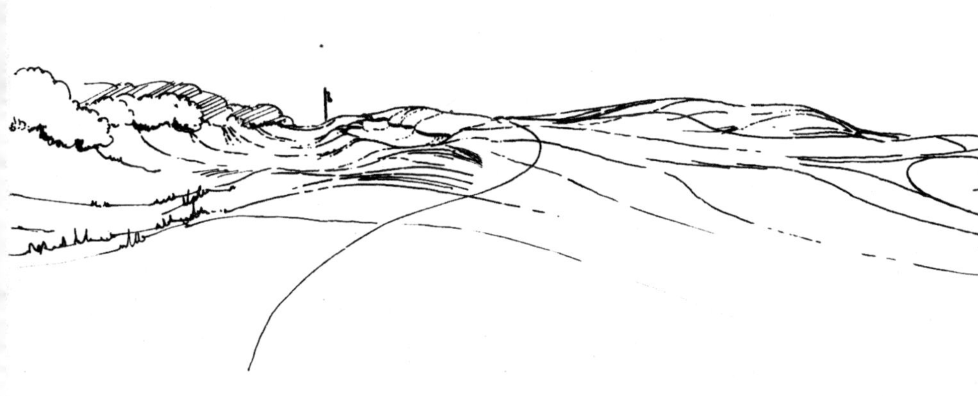

www.olympiapublishers.com
OLYMPIA PAPERBACK EDITION

A CIP catalogue record for this title is
available from the British Library.

ISBN: 978-1-80439-244-7

The information in this book has been compiled by way of
general guidance only. Neither the author nor the publisher shall be
liable or responsible for any loss or damage allegedly arising from
any information or suggestion in this book.

This Edition Published in 2024

Olympia Publishers
Tallis House
2 Tallis Street
London
EC4Y 0AB

Printed in Great Britain

ABOUT THE AUTHOR

A member of the PGA of Canada since 1985 and currently residing in Vancouver, BC, Canada, Scott Minni is a 'Mentor' of the game! His 1996 Canadian Assistants title, 4 BCPGA titles (92,93,94,97) along with his 1999 BCPGA Teacher of the Year award, show that he has worthy credentials. Both of Scott's kids were on golf scholarships and played for Division 1 schools in the USA. Amanda played for Oregon State University (2017-2023) and Jace played for Gonzaga University in Spokane, Washington (2020-2024). The success of both Minni kids along with thousands of Scott's clients, show the long-term success of the Smash & Carve teaching method.

SMASH & CARVE

Golf

The Art of Ball Striking

BY SCOTT MINNI

www.smashandcarve.com

A Tribute to Ben Hogan
1912 ~ 1997

"The ultimate judge of your swing is the flight of the ball"
"You only hit a straight shot by accident, so you had better make it go one way or the other"
"Golf is a game of misses. The person who misses the best is going to win"
~ Ben Hogan

In his day Ben Hogan was dealt some pretty difficult cards. Through hard work and nothing else he rose to the top to become one of the greatest golf legends of all time. I was never fortunate enough to meet Mr Hogan personally but through various books, interviews, and the documentary video, I came to learn that Hogan started in poverty and overcame unbelievable obstacles to reach his goals. It's such a shame that major golf events were not televised until 1954 at the US Open, the year after Hogan had his incredible Triple Slam in 1953. He won all three majors he played in: The Masters, The US Open, and, on his only visit overseas, the British Open. The PGA Championship was to be the fourth major that year, but seeing as how it overlapped with the British Open winning the Grand Slam was not possible.

I write this tribute not only to recognize Hogan's climb to golfing greatness but also to acknowledge his continuous uphill climb from setbacks and bad breaks. This man had good reason to quit many times over. In February, 1949, while driving home from Phoenix, Arizona to Fort Worth, Texas after a tour event, he and his wife Valerie were met head on by a thirty-seven-passenger bus on a foggy Texas highway. Upon impact, Hogan dove across his wife's lap to avoid some of the 20,000 pounds hurtling towards him. Unfortunately, his legs were trapped on the driver's side and were so severely damaged he lived in pain, and with a limp, for the rest of his life. After the historic accident, Hogan was not capable of playing in his regular thirty tournaments per year, instead he played in only five or six. For the rest of Hogan's career, his roster for the golf season would consist of only the Masters, the US Open, Fort Worth's Colonial, the Seminole Amateur-Professional and one or two others. After the accident, Hogan would never again play in the PGA Championship because of its 36-hole match play format. This tournament would be impossible for his battered legs to handle, and the British Open was a one-shot deal in 1953.

Every tournament he played in after the accident would have been excruciating for his battered legs, since the last two rounds were always played on a Saturday; there was no Sunday golf unless a playoff was required! Hogan's courage was clearly demonstrated at the 1950 US Open, just sixteen months after he had nearly been killed. During the third round, at about noon on Saturday, Hogan was nearly leveled by unbearable cramps in his tensor-bandaged legs. "That's it. I just can't make it," he said through clenched teeth to his caddie.

"No Mr. Hogan, you can't quit," the boy had supposedly said. "Because I don't work for quitters." After this Hogan found the strength to carry on and amazingly won the tournament in an eighteen-hole playoff. It didn't end after 36 holes on Saturday – he had to play another round to really earn it, testing his will to the fullest!

8

From what I have come to understand of Ben Hogan, his life had more than its share of disappointment and nothing ever came easy. The accident was one more survival test, a brush with death to add to his already hardened skin as this wasn't his first experience with tragedy. When he was just nine years old his father committed suicide in their home with a gun, and Bennie was in the house. From the age of ten until the age of twenty-eight, for almost eighteen years after his father's death, Hogan lived in poverty.

He turned pro in 1930, at just eighteen. The first ten years of his professional career were disappointing to say the least, he barely made a cheque, yet he kept practicing more than anyone had ever seen. But all the practice wasn't't paying off in those early years, so what could have kept him going? "I just loved to practice," he would say later.

Byron Nelson was a long time friend of Hogan's, going back as far as the 1927 Glen Garden Caddie Tournament, when they were both fifteen. Nelson matured early at golf and enjoyed his most productive years before the age of thirty-four. He retired from full-time play in 1946, the same year Hogan would win his first major. Hogan had to watch his friend Byron enjoy early success at golf, along with financial rewards, while he struggled to scratch out a living. The breakthrough year for Ben Hogan was 1940 when he won his first individual tournament and became the leading money winner. Finally, he was on his way. Again in 1942 he was the leading money winner before the season was stopped halfway through due to the war. This same year the US Open was renamed the Hail America Open and Hogan won the event on the strength of a second round 62. The tournament should have been Hogan's first major. Unfortunately the Hail America was never counted as a major, even though the tournament was identical to a US Open with a winning medal the same as the other four medals he won. Just when life was getting good, setbacks would once again test his spirit. The next year's golf season was canceled due to the war, and Hogan was drafted on March 1, 1943. He would not compete in another major until the 1946 Masters.

Hogan's best years were shortened when you count the three and a half years he lost during the war and the one year he lost due to his accident. Compared to his friend Byron Nelson who was an early bloomer with a real lucky streak, Ben Hogan lost four and a half productive years in his prime, not very encouraging for an already late bloomer. Lucky Byron didn't get drafted, due to a medical reason, and as a result, he enjoyed his historic year of 1945 by winning eighteen times, with eleven in a row, setting a record that will never be broken. Fortunately for Nelson, most of the competitive field, including Hogan, was still in the service for most of that year and there really wasn't much challenge for Nelson. When Hogan got out of the service in August, 1945, one of the first tournaments he played was the Portland Open. Before the tournament Nelson had acquired the nickname 'Mr Golf', but Hogan won the tournament, shooting the lowest seventy-two-hole score in tour history with a 261. His rounds of 65-69-63-64 were two below Nelson's old mark. Jimmy Demaret shook his hand saying, "Congratulations Ben!" To which Hogan flatly remarked, "I guess that takes care of this 'Mr Golf' business."

Hogan achieved his greatness through constant study and practice. "He dug it out of the ground", said Jules Alexander. He prepared for the 1953 Masters at Seminole in Florida with an exhaustive and diligent practice schedule. Six hundred balls before lunch, fifty with each of twelve clubs at three balls per minute, a snack and some rest, and then a repeat of the whole routine in the afternoon. Hogan invented practice. I once heard that he hit balls until his hands would bleed. Others used to laugh at him for practicing because he always out-worked everybody. He was the sole judge of his standards and there wasn't enough daylight in any one day to practice all the shots required for golf. He once stated that every day of practice missed would take him one day longer to be good, and that the more he practiced 'the luckier he got'!

The intensity with which Hogan lived and worked gave rise to these famous quotes, and they have served as motivational tools for many of the world's best golfers over the years. But for all the truth and insight Hogan shared with us on the game, he was perhaps the only man in sports history to have discovered for himself a secret!

THE HOGAN SECRET was unique in the sports world. Where most games relied upon fundamentals and raw skill, golf had a 'Secret' supposedly only known to Hogan. For much of his early career his game was haunted by a nasty hook that kept him up at nights yelling, "Fore left". His Secret to golf ball control was initially introduced to him in March, 1940, by Henry Picard, a respected club pro and tour player who believed in Hogan. On the practice tee after a defeat in the Miami-Biltmore Four Ball Hogan had told Picard, "You told me I was going to be a great player, but I hook too much." Without directly asking for help, Picard knew that Hogan wanted his advice. Instructing Hogan to get his 5-iron, he said 5 minutes together was all they needed. This might have been the first formal lesson Hogan ever took, and the last. In that 5 minutes, Picard simply told Hogan to slice, to turn the left hand weak, aim left and shoot. Interestingly within two weeks after the tip from Picard, Hogan went on a hot streak and won his first individual event, The North and South Golf Championship, following that up with two more consecutive victories. Three wins in a row! Now he believed he could win!

After the early success, Picard's advice gradually wore off and Hogan was back to hooking everything by the time he was drafted into the army in 1942. Perhaps while in the army Hogan really started to understand the full potential of the Picard tip, maybe even adding to it? Whatever he devised during the war certainly must have worked, because when he was discharged in August 1945, he was unstoppable. For the next three and a half years, until the accident in 1949, he won thirty-seven times, including three majors. Throughout the hot streak Hogan began to command attention with his golf game. The media and fellow touring professionals kept asking him, "What's your secret?" "Not telling," he would reply. Hogan refused to comment on his secret, except to confirm that it did indeed exist. Almost ten years to the day of his discharge (from August 1945 to August 1955) he kept everybody guessing. One fellow competitor said, "He just looks like he knows more than the rest of us!"

He finally revealed his Secret in the 1955 August 8 issue of Life Magazine, not surprisingly to widespread disappointment. The Secret simply involved 'anti-hook' swing maneuvers, essentially slicing and fading the ball at will! The public hated it. "What's the fuss," they said, "I already know how to slice!" Basically, his plan was to 'eliminate the left side of the course' using three different swing fundamentals. They were: 1. The weak left-hand grip, rotating the left hand to the left, showing maybe one knuckle when looking down at it; 2. Pronation, while taking the club back he fanned the blade of the club 'open'; 3. Cupping the left wrist inward at the top of the swing and coordinating this move with pronation on the take-away. These three moves when combined together make it virtually impossible to hit a hook.

How ironic that more than ninety per cent of all golfers already own these swing fundamentals. Anyone can slice, and Hogan acknowledged this when he said, "I doubt if it will be worth a doggone to the weekend duffer, and it will ruin a bad golfer." It's probably why he didn't include the information in his classic instructional book, Five Lessons – The Modern Fundamentals of Golf, published in 1957. The best players thought it was brilliant but they were a small percentage. There was no way he was going to include anything regarding the Secret in an instructional book because he knew what the public needed. Commenting on this he stated, "It probably won't be of much help to anyone but the expert player, since most golfers are slicers, and to be an accomplished fader of the ball, one must first know how to draw it." This statement alone is the reason why he only shows 'right to left' mechanics in his book, such as a 'three knuckle, left-hand grip' and 'hit from the inside'. While he never actually mentions ball flight, these fundamentals are just that, right to left.

Hogan was the perfect person to write an instructional book because he figured it all out for himself. He also had a little help along the way, not only from Henry Picard and his advice to slice, but from the lessons he used to teach. He once said, "I think I was a pretty fair teacher, providing the pupil was seriously interested in improving his game. Quite early in my career when I was serving as the professional at the Century Country Club in Purchase, NY, I did a great deal of teaching." As with any instructor today, Hogan probably taught a lot of slicers. Perhaps he combined this teaching experience with the tip from Picard and realized the potential benefits of the slice-swing action. One can only wonder.

Ben Hogan will always serve as an inspiration for many fine players and teachers alike. He was a truly amazing player and instructor, leaving behind a legacy and mystique that has never been surpassed. Hogan's story has achieved legendary status and is still one of the most talked about in the history of golf. Yet in learning more about Mr Hogan, we discover that his legacy was not that mysterious after all. He took sheer will and determination and his passion for golf, and dedicated his life to teaching himself and others how to play their best. Through unbelievably tough work ethics, Ben Hogan figured out for himself a way to achieve his goals both in life and golf, and leaves us with the knowledge and inspiration to do the same.

Credits:

Ben Hogan and 5 *Lessons, The Modern Fundamentals of Golf*
Tiger Woods swing position image page 105

How To Approach A Lesson

Let's get one thing straight before starting — golf is not a natural game and there are no natural golfers! Now, it is true that some individuals are more athletic than others but learning golf is not unlike any other sport or activity you take an interest in; your progress will depend on how much attention you decide to give it. I find it a little amusing when I hear someone say, "Does she ever make it look easy, what a natural." It makes me think that the admirer has no idea as to the time that person spent developing their talent. So it is with golf. To learn it you have to earn it!

All of us golfers share one thing in common, we all started as rookies. I always like to compare learning golf to learning how to play the piano — sure, anyone can play the piano, with two fingers, but how about getting all ten fingers in motion and playing a real piece? This is an acquired skill. Almost always, the admired talent has given their sport or activity plenty of time somewhere in their life, usually during a person's youth (before 18) when responsibilities are minimal. Remember those days, no job, no girlfriend, no husband? This is the most productive learning time for anything, including golf, mainly because there are not a lot of responsibilities getting in the way. Your interest can be number one! Children are not more talented than adults, they just have more time for practice — and practice is the key to golf!

Someone once said, "Golf cannot be taught, it must be learned." That is, if you are serious about improving rapidly, you will naturally be keen to research the game first on your own. You will fast realize that golf is not just a game, it is a lifestyle and is able to provide you with great information, from talking and sharing with other keen players, to watching videos, taking vacations and reading books. This background information will serve as a great foundation as you are learning the mechanics, and will eventually become a part of your game. The more prepared you are before you get to the lesson tee, the greater improvement will be seen.

I have been teaching golf now since 1985 and I have never wished I was in a different line of work. It can, at times, be a little demanding, usually because of a student's lack of enthusiasm towards understanding the theory, and not because of their actual physical performance. I have often wondered if starting my lessons in a classroom setting and initially taking a more theoretical approach would be more beneficial than starting on the range. A new student that is able to communicate with the teacher in the same language will have done some preparation before the lesson and will therefore derive the greatest benefits from it. Reading this text is a great start, for it will prepare you with the phrases and concepts that are common to golfers. Establishing a golf vocabulary early will speed your progress considerably.

Expect awkwardness, because it may not feel right to you when first introduced. Experienced players are often asked to exaggerate a movement or position as part of their development. The exaggerating technique will help you to develop at a much faster rate. In fact, I strongly encourage this method of instruction, since changing muscle memory makes an inch feel like a mile.

SMASH & CARVE IS AN INSTRUCTIONAL BOOK DIVIDED INTO FOUR SECTIONS:

1. Building a swing; 2. Contact; 3. Direction; 4. A final section, Engine Moves, that discusses the magic that happens when the these elements are brought together, a 'whole is greater than the sum of the parts' effect. These four sections, I feel, directly relate to anyone who plays golf. If you are a beginner or a chronic slicer, lesson one will be your starting point followed next by lesson three (direction), then lesson four. My main focus is to get this 'high percentage group' away from 'chronic slicing' as soon as possible. Lesson two (contact) can then be studied and practiced at a much later date, followed lastly by lesson five. If you are quite a seasoned golfer with the ability to draw/hook the golf ball on command (chronic hooker not chronic slicer), you are welcome to study and practice this book in order. While doing so I want you to ask yourself this question: "Do I need help with my contact or direction?" I guarantee it will be one or the other, if not both. This is not about what you're doing wrong – that doesn't matter. It's about knowing what's right for you and your game. As a lifetime golfer you will always be working on contact or direction, hence, the title of this book... Smash & Carve. Too many players spend time trying to achieve distance. I purposely leave this area alone because if you can achieve skillful contact and direction, distance will naturally develop as a result.

My thoughts for developing this text have been inspired by every lesson, and there have been many over the years. The extensive research I have gathered, combined with constant tinkering in my own game, have contributed greatly to, and inspired, the development of Smash & Carve. What I want to address is the incredible similarity of trouble patterns that influence a high majority of golfers. These trouble patterns consist mostly of trying to scoop or pick the ball off the ground, and in trying to create straight shots – scoop and straight or pick and straight, versus Smash & Carve. These are very different 'styles' of play. Smash & Carve is the ultimate; this style can play anywhere, good lie or bad, wind or no wind. Pick and straight can play pretty well at times, but struggles with bad lies and trouble shots. scoop and straight used by the game's worst players will struggle forever! Smash & Carve is contact and direction. The sole purpose of the swing motion is to develop and perfect, to some degree, these two principle areas in your game. There are two ways to learn and build a golf game;, from the swing to the ball, or from the ball to the swing. I want you to build from the BALL-TO-THE-SWING to ensure that FUNCTION AND STYLE are always working together to guarantee steady progress.

lesson 1

Building a Swing

Summary

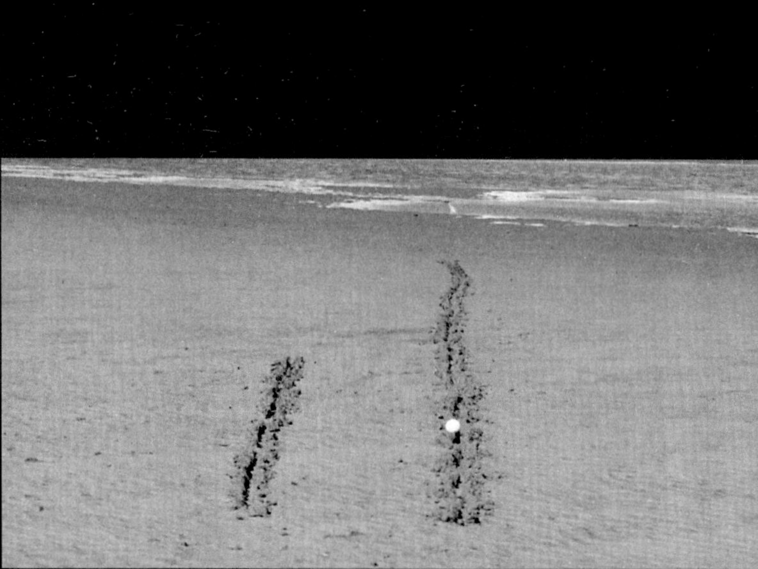

The fundamentals introduced throughout this lesson are the basics. All golfers should be encouraged to learn and develop the basics, regardless of how long it takes for them to feel comfortable. This will ensure a player's progress is always moving forward. When a golfer fails to learn the basics completely their progress can become entangled with bad habits that set in, slowing advancement to the next level.

The purpose of this first lesson is to introduce and explore the essential positions and movements in the golf swing. They are: 1. the Grip; 2. the Set-up; 3. the Backswing; and 4. the Unloading Sequence. If you consider yourself a player with some experience feel free to skip this lesson and move on to the lesson that applies to you the most. This lesson may be helpful to you later if you need review. If you're a new golfer with limited experience, it is very important to practice and repeat these basics. Practicing at home (in front of a mirror) with or without a club (similar to shadow boxing) ensures that good habits are being memorized before you begin hitting balls at a driving range.

If a particular position feels awkward or uncomfortable at first, don't panic, this initial discomfort is quite normal. Constant repetition will ensure these new-found habits become natural. The more you can practice the better. Be a keener! Eventually these basics will provide you with a dependable foundation to build on in the upcoming lessons.

The Grip

THE LEFT HAND

Before you establish your left hand position, the clubface must be square or perpendicular to the intended target line. (figure 1).

First: Place your left hand on the club making sure the clubface stays in a square position. Extend your left thumb down the grip so it is stretched out (long thumb). Turn your hand slightly to your right so you can see 3 knuckles while looking down (figure 1).

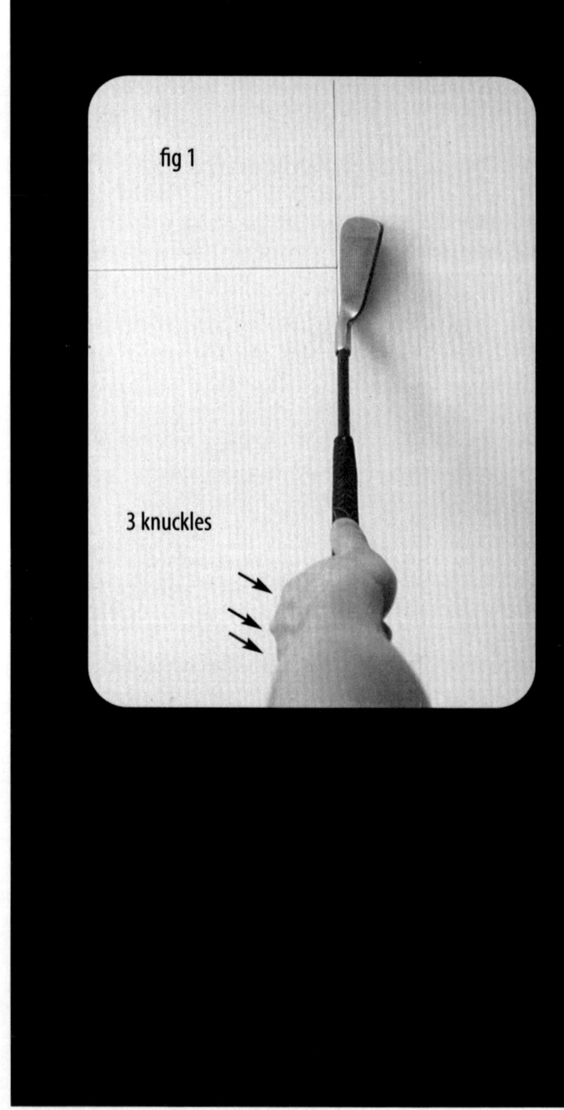

THE RIGHT HAND

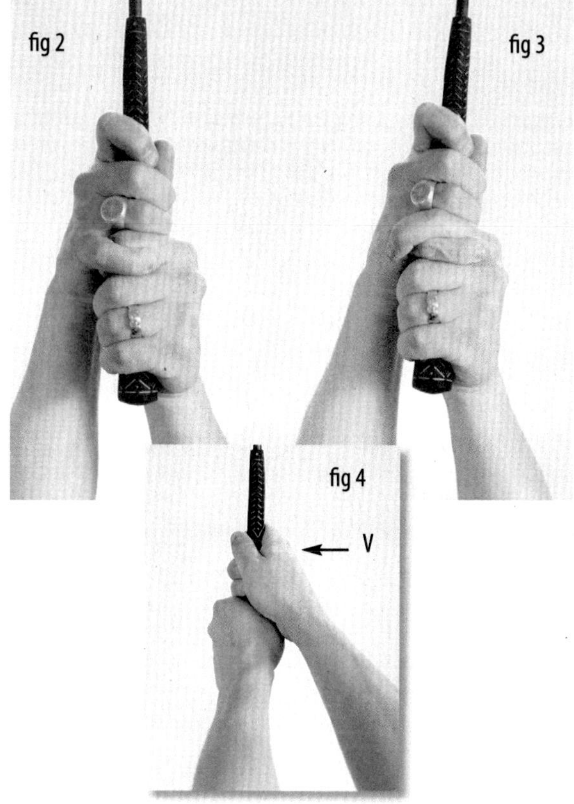

Next: overlap (figure 2) or interlock (figure 3) the right pinky finger with the left forefinger.

Your right hand will complete the grip by closing itself over the thumb on your left hand; the left hand thumb should be completely hidden by the right hand (figure 4). The 'V' of your right hand should point to your chin.

NOTE: The key point when establishing your right hand is to hold the club more in the fingers rather than in the palm. This finger hold will allow the completion of the grip to be easily achieved although it may feel awkward for a short time. This initial awkwardness is almost always felt when a golfer insists on remaining strong with their right hand rather than accepting the left hand as dominant. Good golf requires that the left hand be in control, therefore, if the right hand initially feels loose and insecure it's a good sign.

The Set-up

The completed set-up from the front angle (figure 5) should consist of:

1. Feet slightly wider than your shoulders.

2. Right foot straight, left foot slightly open (25 degrees approx.).

3. Left arm straight and in line with the club shaft.

4. Right arm bent in toward your stomach.

Ball location will depend on whether you are using an iron club or a wood (figure 6). All iron clubs should be based in the center or back in the stance. All woods should be based 2 inches inside the left heel with a slightly wider stance.

In general, longer clubs should be played with a slightly wider stance, and shorter clubs with a slightly narrower stance. Eventually through experience your stance will become more personalized, especially in close to the green. For now, the basics shown above will be sufficient.

The completed set-up from the back angle (figure 7) should consist of:

1. Posture

   - bending from the waist approximately 30 degrees

   - knees slightly bent, but still tall

   - butt out, back quite straight

2. Hand position; 6 to 8 inches from your left thigh.

All golf clubs are different lengths so it will be necessary to adjust your distance from the ball. Your posture and hand position (figure 7) should remain constant regardless of how long or short the club is. Simply back up or move closer depending on the chosen club, keeping your hands 6 - 8 inches from the left thigh. Do not stand taller for longer clubs or crouch over for shorter ones. Make your consistent posture the strength of your set-up.

The Swing Motion

The swing motion consists of: the backswing, the downswing, and the follow-through. Each of these areas need to be treated separately during the developmental stages. As you practice and develop these swing positions you will need to think of your body as two separate sections consisting of INNER PARTS and OUTER PARTS.

The INNER PARTS are: the trunk, feet, legs, hips, chest and head.

The OUTER PARTS are (ghosted on the photos above): the shoulders, arms, hands and the golf club.

The backswing sequence will be dominated by the outer parts, mainly the arms.

The downswing sequence will be dominated by the inner parts, mainly the hips.

Centrifugal Force

The foundation of the golf swing is based on centrifugal force. The spinning and uncoiling action from the body will multiply to the arms, then multiply again to the clubhead. For instance, if the hips uncoil at 40mph the arms will travel at 60mph and the clubhead at approximately 80mph. The greater the pulling action from the hips (inner parts) and the transfer of weight, the better. This is true for power and control because the arms will have a powerful force (hips) leading them into position.

fig 9

Note: Because centrifugal force is imperative to the swing, I suggest you strengthen your back and stomach. Keep your power center healthy and strong with a stretching program, abdominal exercises (i.e. sit-ups) and back strengthening exercises. Remember, the most important piece of equipment is your body!

The Backswing

The 'loading of the backswing' as it is commonly referred to, is best understood with a heavy emphasis on the word LOADING. When the backswing is done correctly it will load the golfer into a 'spring effect' position. This loaded position is created by a straight left arm (outer parts) that travels much further back than do the hips (inner parts). Loaded means the hips are ready to fire or lead the downswing, that's why you don't want your hips to turn very much on the backswing. Indirectly you will be giving your hips a head start by only turning them a fraction of the shoulder turn.

The swing motion begins with a strong set-up position (figure 10) with your left arm dominant and in line with the club shaft. The initial takeaway to the 1/4 position (figure 11) should be dominated with the outer parts, your left arm maintaining dominance (straight). Subtle wrist action to this 1/4 position is two-fold: 1. to fan the clubface open slightly, where the clubface points to the sky (circled in figure 11), and; 2. to hinge slightly. The inner parts, mainly the hips, remain quite still to this position.

When moving from the 1/4 position to the 1/2 position (figure 12) the left arm must continue its dominance (straight). Your wrists are free to hinge more than shown in figure 12 (club shaft vs. left arm is 40° approximate, but I suggest less wrist break rather than more. Your feet should still be flat on the ground, with minimum hip turn (inner parts very quiet).

The completed backswing (figure 13) can stop at approximately the 3/4 position (notice the clubshaft vs. my left arm showing a 90° angle). This is considered to be a complete backswing. Having your left arm travel further past this point will not create extra distance, instead it may decrease your chances for consistency.

The most critical point in the backswing is at the 1/2 position. This is a check point for many advanced players. By setting the club correctly at the 1/2 position, the 3/4 position can then be easily achieved for all body types.

A full backswing (left arm pointing straight up to the sky) is not advisable because of the extra flexibility that is required. Remember, bigger is not necessarily better during the backswing.

The Unloading Sequence

The unloading sequence consists of the downswing and the follow-through. The change of direction must be dominated with your inner parts. You can spin your hips to the left, or use your right or left leg as a driving force, but whichever you choose, a part of your lower body must initiate the downswing to create the necessary pulling effect that is called centrifugal force. Avoid dominating the unloading process with any of your outer parts for it will only create big problems that lead to even worse habits.

Once the backswing position has been established (figure 14) the unloading sequence can then take place.

The hips (inner parts) are the largest and most powerful part of your body, therefore leading the downswing with the spinning action of your hips will allow your arm swing (outer parts) to drop into a position called the slot (figure 15). The slot is quite close to your right hip and can only be accessed through the correct sequence of movement. On the downswing the inner parts lead and the outer parts follow (refer to pages 24 and 25).

The follow-through occurs after the ball has been hit, and requires a strong spinning action of the hips combined with the extension of both arms down the target line. Follow through means you swing at the target or down the line. When more power is applied to the shot your arms will travel farther up toward your head.

The only point in the swing where both arms are straight is at the 1/4 follow-through position (figure 16), which is 2 to 3 feet past impact. The left arm remains straight to this point and the right arm follows suit.

At the 3/4 follow-through position your right arm should remain quite straight (figure 17). Your left arm will begin to fold or bend as the swing nears completion.

Casting

Directly related to the downswing is a common error in movement known as casting. Its cause originates in the first part of the downswing.

Casting means the golfer uncocks the wrists during the downswing (figure 19), thereby failing to control the downswing sequence with their inner parts. Feeling compelled, the player feverishly tries to hit the ball with the clubhead (outer parts). The player casts the clubhead out and away from their body, breaking the correct sequence by not leading the downswing with the lower body spin which, in turn, opens the door to numerous errors. Casting is used when fishing, not golfing, and is an extremely harmful habit that you need to be aware of in the early stages of your development.

At the end of lesson 2 hand action will be covered more extensively. At this point it's not imperative that you master the correct movement, however you should become familiar with the downswing sequence and the leading action of the lower body spin. Remember that dominating the downswing with the hands and wrists can be disastrous.

fig 18

fig 19

The Power Swing

Your power swing will consist of a 3/4 backswing with a full follow-through. 3/4 to full.

Greater power is not achieved by increasing your backswing past this 3/4 position (figure 20). Although there are many fine players who do, the fact is bigger is not necessarily better!

It is not surprising that a lot of players are almost always concerned with generating more power, but actually golf should be understood as a control game and the premium should be placed on consistency. Everyone has the flexibility to develop a solid 3/4 backswing. Going past this point will not help your consistency or your distance. Balancing the 3/4 follow-through with the 3/4 backswing would be just fine. If you have a lot of acceleration in your unloading process stopping at 3/4 is not advisable. There are many women who can swing over 70 mph and men that can swing over 90 mph, therefore, a full follow-through where both arms are bent as the club ends up behind your head (figure 21) is likely to develop. This will depend on how aggressive your nature. Your arms should eventually fold at the follow-through, but not until you are beyond the 3/4 position.

The Game... In Short

In addition to the power swing there are also touch swings that are used to control distance, especially from 100 yards in and around the green. During a round of golf you will encounter different situations that need creativity, especially when distance control is required. You can develop your short game most effectively by learning and practicing 3 touch swings.

There are a wide range of specialty shots in the short game but in this text we will concentrate our efforts on the 1/4 to 1/4, 1/2 to 1/2 and 3/4 to 3/4 swings. Unlike the power swing, the short shot requires the follow-through to mirror the backswing, balancing back to forth. If you take the club back 1/4way, you follow-through 1/4 way. This is true for the 1/2 and 3/4 swings as well.

The smaller the swing, the shorter distance the ball will travel. As you begin to practice this skill you will also develop a feel that you can rely upon to discern distance. Depending on how the ball is struck a 1/4 swing might produce a 25 yard shot, a 1/2 swing a 50 yard shot and a 3/4 length might hit the ball 75 yards. You will develop feel and consistency through practice and repetition. Eventually, with experience you will be able to control distance through 5 yard increments, 5, 10, 15, 20, etc. Building a repertoire of swing lengths will prepare you for good shot-making at any distance.

quarter to quarter

half to half

three-quarter to three-quarter

Summary

During this lesson we have been developing your basic fundamentals for golf. Do not treat these fundamentals lightly as they will be with you for the rest of your life! I cannot emphasize enough the importance of practicing these basics at home, indoors or outdoors, while watching television, standing in front of a mirror, with or without a club. Go ahead, be a keener, the more the better! You don't have to be at a driving range to be learning and developing your game.

There are many students that I see in a golf season who do not have the basics established in their muscle memory, therefore improving their game will be a constant struggle because they will always be fighting bad habits. Try to be patient while you learn this multi-faceted game. It requires everyone to learn at a slow and accurate rate so the good habits can develop and become a part of you – to be natural. You can't be in a hurry to learn golf because it takes a lot of time, which is why the best players learned their games while they were young. The main reason kids can improve faster than adults is because they have few responsibilities apart from school and homework. They have all the time to practice and play – what a life! Adults have trouble finding the time between demanding work schedules, spouses and kids. Golf takes patience, practice and time... positive results need to be earned.

Now that you have a good understanding of the basics introduced in this lesson, we will continue to build on these skills in lessons 2 and 3. Lesson 2 (Smash) gives purpose to the swing and explains the technique and importance of contacting the ball properly. Lesson 3 (Carve) explains the shot control focusing on direction. As we move forward, always remember to practice what you've learned in lesson 1 for it is your first step to a successful swing.

Practice...

...Anywhere

...Anytime

CONTACT

STEP **5** BALL LOCATION
STEP **6** HAND ACTION

DELAYING VS CASTING

Summary

This lesson will expand on the hitting area, or the impact zone with an iron club. If you are a fairly new golfer, or a chronic slicer, I suggest you skip forward to chapter 3 (direction) before working with this chapter on contact. The reason is because most golfers need to develop a 'right to left shot' (draw/hook) first, whereby the 'inside out' swing path is pretty much second nature. In my experience, it is virtually impossible to teach a chronic slicer how to hit down on the ball properly because of their outside-in swing path.

During this lesson I will refer to the word SOLID, frequently. It is imperative that you understand this specific word and its meaning as described in this lesson. Solid is the pleasure of the game, the addiction. It is the 'sweet' result of skillful ball striking, the pot at the end of the rainbow. When a golfer can rely on hitting solid shots every time, the game becomes much more enjoyable because consistency has been achieved. Then, distance can be controlled because the ball is being struck consistently, the same way, every time.

IT'S NOT THE DRIVE, IT'S HOW YOU ARRIVE. Many golfers in today's game are so hung up on hitting the big drive that they disregard the importance of being a solid ball-striker. They think that their driver is the most important club in their bag, when actually the iron clubs are much more significant. That's why there are more irons than woods in a set of clubs. When a golfer learns how to hit their irons solid, the woods will then be easy to learn. This lesson will concentrate on iron play.

To achieve proficient ball-striking abilities you will have to focus on impact and the ball to ground relationship. Learning good ball-striking from the ground up will teach you how your golf swing can produce these solid shots. Without a clear understanding of how the ground relates to impact, even a good swing can produce a picking or scooping action. It is crucial that you build both elements of swing and impact together, thereby achieving SOLID CONTACT.

Scan the QR code
to watch a
1 minute
Smash & Carve
demonstration!

SCAN ME

fig 1   fig 2

These sequence photos show myself using a 7 iron (figures 1 to 4), and I have just hit a solid shot. Notice how the ball and turf are leaving the hitting area. There is certainly a lot of action happening here. Pay particular attention to the angle of the club shaft (figure 2). Notice how it has a backward lean, as my hands are staying out in front of the clubhead.

There are many different sayings or phrases that describe this action of Impact you see here. HIT DOWN AND THROUGH, COMPRESS THE BALL, or DE-LOFT THE CLUB.

All of these phrases effectively describe impact and the hitting area. They are swing-thoughts that have been used by many fine players over the years.

The action of impact has varying degrees of aggressiveness and has been described as 'controlled violence'. The size of the divot will depend on certain variables such as the amount of power supplied, the club used, and the condition of the turf. If the shot was only hit 20 yards, the divot will always be quite small. If the club used was a 3 iron from 200 yards, the divot will also be somewhat small. If it was a 9 iron from 140 yards off very wet turf, as is often the case on the west coast, the divot will be huge! Lofted clubs such as 8 iron, 9 iron and wedge tend to take bigger, deeper divots than less lofted clubs. The size of the divot will vary but there will be only one impact position you are to develop.

The next time you watch a golf tournament on television notice how every player takes divots with their irons. The single most important factor concerning hitting solid shots is taking divots! All good players take them, after they have hit the ball, yet this crucial maneuver goes relatively unnoticed during a player's early years in golf. I want you to learn how the ball gets into the air first, then build the swing fundamentals. In other words, build from the ball to the swing.

My Story Of Solid

I remember vividly the day I discovered how to strike solid shots, the events of which make for an interesting story to share with you. Before continuing, I would like you to keep in mind that I was only 18 years old at the time of this story, and not yet weighed down by the responsibilities of the work world, had a lot of personal time available.

One hot summer afternoon at the old University Golf Course practice fairway, I was practicing alone, wearing out my shag balls with sweaty determination and chasing a dream. I had been playing golf for about 8 years, and a typical summer golf day often lasted from dawn till dusk, hitting as many as a thousand balls. This particular day was, to put it mildly, not going well at all. Disgusted with the way I was striking the ball, my mood turned dark, calling myself every bad name I could think of. Thinking I was useless and pathetic, I lost my temper and started to hit right down on the ball, trying to break my club on it and rip out a huge piece of turf. I would put the ball way back in my stance and smash down on it as hard as possible.

Funny how anger is often a turning point in life, suddenly revealing answers we have struggled for so long to find. Like a silver lining on a very dark cloud, I couldn't believe what started to happen. In absolute awe, I watched shot after shot start with a powerful low trajectory and rise gracefully toward the horizon, reaching its peak before falling to the earth. The whole experience was incredible; I was no longer thinking about swing mechanics, just hitting the ball with a substantial, descending blow. A real smashing action!

All was not yet perfect though. At that time my idol was Jack Nicklaus. I tried to imitate everything he did in his golf game, paying particular attention to the mechanics of the swing. Two very important fundamentals he used: 1. Keep your head still, and 2. Play every shot off your left heel. Up to this time, I used these swing keys religiously, practicing and playing every day. Now, suddenly, I found myself in quite a dilemma. If I played the ball off my left heel and kept my head still as Mr Nicklaus suggested, I could not hit the ball Solid every time but if I played the ball back in my stance and just hit down on the ball I could ~ what was going on?

Two years later I found my answer when I was introduced to George Knudson and his theories. In contrast to Jack Nicklaus, Mr Knudson recommended playing the ball in different locations for different irons rather than always off the left heel. He also recommended allowing your head to move during the swing, rather than attempting to keep it still! This was wonderful news! While I had already figured this out for myself it confirmed that my discovery was right on track. If I had had a clear understanding of impact from the beginning, I could have saved myself a lot of time, maybe 5 years. This is exactly what I am trying to do for you — save you time. To help you move forward not backwards.

There will always be different teaching programs that endorse a variety of concepts. However, one truth will always remain: Good golf absolutely demands SOLID BALL STRIKING. Do you hit solid shots with the swing mechanics you use now?

Definitions

Study the definitions below. This is the correct terminology used in describing the contact within the game of golf. Their meanings indicate how (not where) a golfer hits a shot.

SOLID: The Collins English Language Dictionary describes something that is solid as having all its individual pieces very close together so there is no space between them.

In golf, the iron club strikes down on the ball, hitting the ball first (solid) then tearing out turf, past the ball, after the ball.

THIN: The iron strikes the ball only, without any turf. (An error – but is the most productive error. "Thin to win" they say).

FAT: The iron strikes the turf before the ball. (An error)

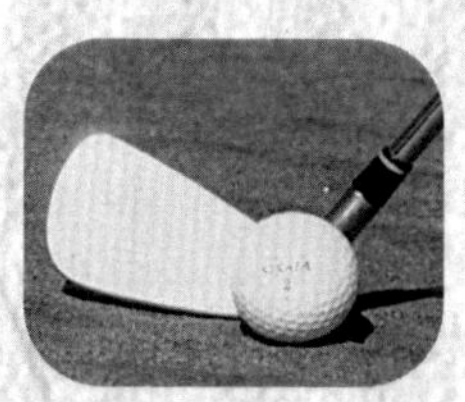

SHANK: The iron strikes the ball on the shaft, or the heel area of the club. (An error).

** Toe shots are so rare I have decided not to include them here.*

It is imperative that you memorize and understand these 4 words and their meanings. Without this knowledge your ability to evaluate and communicate your performance is virtually impossible. The following pages are a guide/program toward SOLID ball-striking – these steps deal directly with hitting SOLID shots, not with where the ball goes. This we will learn in lesson 3.

When learning how to strike a golf ball SOLID you must first have the correct impression and vision that deals with the golf club and shaft angle at Impact.

Let's review some important phrases:

Down and Through - hit the ball on the way down, taking the divot after.

Compress the Ball - getting the clubface to push the ball against the ground.

Deloft the Club - hit the ball with your hands ahead of the clubhead.

These three technique phrases describe the same intention — to hit SOLID shots. They also describe a low trajectory. When trying to achieve solid contact you basically have to like hitting the ball on a lower than normal trajectory (hands ahead of the ball). A good golf swing will tend to push the ball out to the target. The loft will then supply the appropriate trajectory. Good ball-strikers get the ball out to the target very fast — they compress the ball against the ground and extend it out to the target all in the same motion.

Figure 5 shows how the clubhead first contacts the golf ball. The initial contact should be (envisioned) in the middle of the ball. Notice how the shaft is leaning to my left, emphasizing delofting with my hands moderately ahead of the ball. Figure 6 shows where the clubhead first contacts the ground. Notice how the initial contact is after the ball. The clubhead will then go even further past the ball, tearing out turf as much as 12 to 15 inches past the ball (figure 7). If the hands are not leading the clubhead through the hitting area, taking a divot after the ball is virtually impossible. Let's think for a moment how backspin is created. When the club strikes down on the ball it pinches the ball and compresses it against the ground, the ball then spins out from its compression, riding up the grooves on the clubface producing backspin. The amount of backspin will then depend on 'how much power' and 'what club was used'. There will always be backspin, you don't even have to try for it. A golf shot will never have topspin.

Figure 8 shows how most golfers perceive the hitting area. They try to scoop the ball up. Many believe the higher the shot, the more backspin — this is not the case.

Your first step is to have the correct impression of impact before proceeding to step #2.

Key Thoughts

Before we look at the golf swing itself and the essentials required to achieve Solid Contact, I would like you to understand that 'taking divots' with every iron shot you ever hit is imperative! Unfortunately, most golf facilities in areas where the game is seasonal only allow golfers to hit practice balls from mats — talk about different! You play the game off grass yet you have to practice off mats! If the thought of hitting the ground is not at the top of your list, it will always be difficult to hit the ball solid and experience the pleasure of it. As your ball striking improves you will learn to appreciate and eventually enjoy striking the ground and taking divots. Reinforce this point weekly by watching golf on television. If the best players take divots, why shouldn't you?

It's important to note that power is not required at this point in time. The easiest way to build proper contact and become a better player is by practicing smaller shots that are inside 100 yards — pitching and chipping. This will allow your body to absorb the impact of a golf shot without risking injury to yourself. Do not disregard the importance of practicing the short game more than your power game; don't forget that the point of the game is to get the ball in the hole!

1/4 to 1/4 and 1/2 to 1/2. These swings are as big as you will need to start developing proper contact. The larger your swing gets, the more difficult hitting solid shots will become. Power has its place in the game, but remember that consistency is the key to improving. Learning the game from your short shots is a win-win situation; you will develop your short game and become a solid ball-striker. The full-swing is a mere extension of the 1/2 swing, the ball-striking basics are the same. There is only one description of proper contact, whether it be a 10 yard shot with a pitching wedge or a 180 yard shot with a 5 iron, the shots get hit the exact same way — SOLID!

The image below shows a divot pattern after 100 balls have been hit with a 7-iron. The grid illustration shows the order with which the pattern is created. Taking pride in your divot pattern will promote consistency in your ball-striking and is easily repaired.

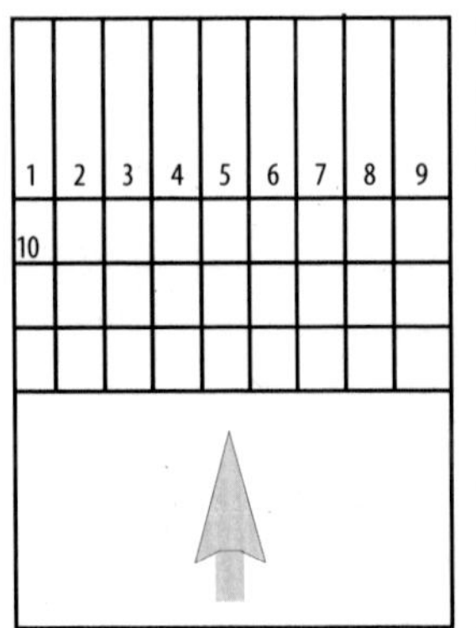

Step 2 ~ Footwork *the weight-shift*

When hitting Solid golf shots a player must dominate the swing motion with the inner parts. The weight-shift (inner parts) is the foundation of any good golf swing and must be the dominant force before attention can be focused on the arms and hands. Many struggling golfers dominate the golf swing with their arms and don't use nearly enough hips and legs during the unloading process.

When loading the backswing (figure 9) your feet should stay flat on the ground (don't lift your left heel). Your h should be minimal, with only a slight weight-shift right. By keeping your feet flat on the ground, you will be 'coiling' or loading. You might feel a little s in your lower back caused by your feet staying flat ground. This stiffness is necessary, that's what is by 'loading'; you load up your right side, readyir spring forward.

When unloading the downswing and follow-throuç hips and your legs must go first. The center, which i nated by the weight-shift and spinning action of yo (figure 10), will pull your arms through the hitting area and into the follow-through (figure 11). Notice the complete turn of the hips to face the target.

In my opinion, if there was a most important move in the golf swing it would have to be the weight-shift. There has to be a dominant force in the swing motion, and that dominant force is controlled by the weight-shift.

fig 9

fig 10

fig 11

Don't Keep Your Head Down

As your body weight shifts naturally and aggressively to your left foot do not keep your head down, in fact, this swing thought should be banished from the game. It will only hinder progress, not help it! Annika Sorenstam of the LPGA Tour and David Duval of the PGA Tour have been helpful examples of just how early a player can lift their head once they have hit the ball. They keep their heads quite still on the back-swing, but on the downswing and follow-through they appear to be leading with their face and lifting their head almost before contact. This type of swing action is just wonderful because it dismisses that age old rule that 'you have to keep your head down'. Not only will this tip limit your progress and make you feel and look completely unnatural, it is very damaging to your back and neck muscles (figure 13).

Practice becoming more of a TALL PLAYER. The strength and grace of a good swing comes from being tall. Lift your head right after you hit it, and stand very tall at the follow-through. It is still very possible to take divots and be tall, it just requires practice.

This 'old school' cliché is also not in agreement with modern kinesthetic knowledge; it won't help your swing and you could injure yourself – don't be influenced by it.

Step 3 ~ Arm Extension

The downswing to slightly post-impact is considered the 'moment of truth'. Our efforts will concentrate on this 'attack of the ball'.

At impact 90% of your body weight must be on your left foot showing the domination from the weight-shift (figure 14). Your left arm should still be quite straight, your right arm slightly bent.

fig 14

Your left arm should continue to drive through the hitting area, staying ahead of your right arm. This left arm extension will help to provide the 'divot action' after impact (figure 15).

The left arm is in control of the post-impact extension from both arms. If the left arm is extending down the line, the right can't help but extend also. The left arm must always dominate the right, which might be the reason why the glove is worn on the left hand.

Down and Through describes a technique that should be practiced religiously. This swing thought can single handedly promote ball striking excellence and make the solid shot a consistent part of your game.

fig 15

fig 16

Note: the slight backward bend of the left wrist in figure 16 is a result of the action called supination. When combined with the left arm extension, it will lengthen the hitting area tremendously. Supination is discussed at length in lesson 4.

Don't Stay Behind The Ball

When extending your left arm out toward the target, thus taking your divots after the ball, you may lose your balance toward the target from time to time (figure 17). If this happens don't panic, it's not as bad as you might think. In losing your balance toward the target you are reinforcing the thought of taking the divot after the ball.

Gary Player has been an excellent example over the years of a great player that doesn't stay behind the ball, in fact he actually takes a couple of steps toward the target after hitting the ball. If anything, he falls forward, getting his entire body weight into the shot. It's a wonderful swing move to imitate.

Ideally, at the completion of the swing (figure 18) you would like to be standing straight up, over your left foot, facing the target with perfect balance.

Avoid the loathsome 'C-Back' (figure 19). This position is commonly achieved by players that believe in either keeping their head still throughout the swing, or staying behind the ball. You can probably imagine from the photo that this is not a very comfortable position. Please protect your back and neck area. Swing healthy!

Step 4 ~ The Arc

The back and forward arc of the swing motion will be different on either side of the ball.

On the backswing (figure 20, solid line) the left arm arc should be quite wide. Your left arm extension should be full, away from your body, keeping the inner parts quite still.

On the downswing (figure 21, dotted line) the arc should shrink somewhat. Your arms should be pulled into your body slightly, as your weight-shift begins to pull your arms down. On the downswing, your arms should get considerably closer to your body, creating a steeper descending angle than that of the backswing.

On the follow-through (figure 22) the arc will extend out again, just like the backswing. This arc change only reaffirms the swing key of 'down and through'.

In short, the swing arc should be: wide, then shallow, then wide.

When practicing the swing arc and the previous steps, remember the eventual goal of hitting 'SOLID SHOTS' and taking divots after the ball.

Key Thoughts

Before continuing, I would like to share some interesting perceptions of contact that many golfers have. One of my main goals of this text is to put forth a clear understanding of impact and how the ball gets into the air. A clear majority of all golfers I teach in a season have very similar perceptions of impact and most of the time these perceptions are damaging. Here are a few examples:

- I'M AIMING TO HIT THE GROUND JUST BEFORE THE BALL
- THE CLUB SCOOPS AND LIFTS THE BALL INTO THE AIR
- I MUST GET UNDER IT

These thoughts are very damaging; they have nothing to do with hitting solid shots. They are opposites of the 'down and through' action you are learning. If you relate to statements such as these, I firmly believe it will be impossible to develop solid contact because misdirected statements such as these will stop your learning curve from moving forward.

These types of evaluation statements are so popular with the average golfing population it's no wonder over 80% of all golfers shoot over 100! If you are a fairly new golfer you don't have to feel bad, these damaging statements are made even by decent players with over 10 years of experience.

Make sure that statements you make are accurate in explaining your shots and your game. If I heard a student of mine say, "I'm just not getting under it." it would always be a struggle for that student to improve. Almost every student I teach is simply amazed when I hit an iron shot and show them the divot after the ball, they can't believe it. It seems to be information that isn't being talked about nearly enough. So remember, hit down on the ball with a descending blow and take the divot after the ball — DOWN AND THROUGH!

Step 5 ~ Ball Location

As you gain more experience with golf you will find that 'where' you place the ball in relation to your stance is an ongoing process, there are no absolutes, there are only recommendations. The more advanced your game, the more variations in ball location. I will give you a base to work from, but also encourage you to experiment.

The main difference in a set of golf clubs is between woods and irons. The woods are designed to sweep the ball into the air, where the irons are designed to take divots. It is because of this design difference, that your ball location should change. A standard ball location for hitting woods is 2 inches inside your left heel (figure 23) or forward in your stance. A standard ball location for hitting irons is the center of your stance (figure 24).

Because in this lesson we are not dealing with hitting woods, I will encourage you to experiment with putting the ball back in your stance with your irons. Try placing the ball 2 inches right of center, then 4 inches right of center, then 6 inches right of center, etc. Notice how different ball locations create different trajectories — have fun while you experiment.

fig 23

fig 24

Step 6 ~ Wrist Action

Before we get into step 6, I would like you to understand that the correct hand action (wrist action) is developing in your swing motion as a result of studying and practising the previous 5 steps. If you feel that your contact is improving, then you need not practice this step at this time.

The essential elements for correct hand action during the swing motion

1. Understanding the word Solid and how the clubhead must deloft at impact.

2. The weight-shift moving forward to your left foot must be strong enough to assist the delofting process.

3. The left arm extension must drive down and through, down the line, not up at the sky.

4. The arc must shrink as the downswing begins, the left arm extension should be quite wide going back, then on the downswing the arc will get considerably closer to the body, before extending away from the body again after Impact.

5. Ball location will affect the delofting process.

Our final step is to train the wrists to lag the clubhead during the downswing. This final step deals with 'backward momentum'. The clubhead must stay behind the hands at impact in order to maximize the velocity of speed through the hitting zone. If the clubhead catches up to the hands at any point in the downswing the 'stored up power' will be lost and a nasty scooping action will develop.

While you are developing flowing hand action it is very important to be aware of when and where the wrist break is needed. On the backswing very little wristbreak is needed; wrist action is needed in the downswing just before impact. Basically, more delay means more power.

Figure 28 demonstrates how the wrists remain delayed until they reach the golf ball. This 'late release' must be trusted in the early going as shots flying high to the right should be expected. The correct lagging action from the wrist combined with a strong weight shift to your left foot creates the stored up power that propels the ball. This delay action when combined with the backward bend from the clubshaft (backward momentum) will deliver maximum clubhead speed.

DELAY THE HIT, WAIT FOR IT — these swing keys explain the lagging action. When the weight-shift is strong to the left foot and the wrists are delaying on the downswing you will be amazed at how far you are able to hit a ball.

This particular swing move is considered by many to be very frustrating. Because the clubhead gets sort of 'left behind' many will panic, they feel a sense of 'not knowing where the clubhead is'. Actually, the clubhead will be where it should be — following your body, arms and hands. The swing is a 'chain reaction of movement'.

The lagging action is not only necessary for power and control reasons, it will also apply to your short shots in close to the green. Also known as soft hands, the lagging action is needed for touch as well.

Delaying vs Casting

Errors have a way of creating a dominos effect in the golf swing, and casting is no exception. Often originating with an incorrect perception of impact, casting relates to getting under the ball and scooping (figure 32). Notions of having to retrace the swing arc, back and down, and not getting off the right side through impact, can both be isolated causes of casting. Casting often develops out of a combination of bad habits. It completely opposes the 'lagging action' that is necessary to create the proper flow and delay from the wrists during the downswing (figures 29 & 30).

On the previous page notice the near 70° wrist break in figure 26 (top of backswing). If the wrists unhinge on the downswing (figure 31) there wouldn't have been much point in hinging them to begin with. This would mean the wrists hinged and unhinged before the ball was hit, resulting in two unnecessary moves.

Casting is defeating the purpose of using equipment that will flex. By attempting to hit down and through on all iron shots you will remove most of the tendencies to cast. Stay clear of this frequent error common among pickers and scoopers.

Summary

Contact is such a necessary element in the game of golf, first because it gets the ball airborne and second because it allows the player to control the distance. Controlling the distance is the essence of the game. The result of good contact is 'SOLID' and this should apply to all the irons, short game included. SOLID is set out for you to learn and earn by focusing on this lesson, but while practicing you may find yourself falling prey to a vicious circle that involves hitting fat and thin shots alternately. Here's an example: if you happen to hit a few fat shots while practicing don't assume that you've hit too much ground — you've actually hit too far behind the ball. Because you fear gouging too much earth again you are apt to hit the next shot thin, intentionally avoiding the ground. This is the vicious circle: fat, thin, fat, thin etc. They are opposites of each other.

By providing you with a clear understanding of the importance of 'impact', and giving you the goal of 'SOLID', you should now be able to apply these steps to a practice program and ready yourself for mastering this lesson; it shows you how to achieve the true objective... to SMASH! Now, on to... CARVE!

lesson 3

Direction

In this lesson we will explore the DIRECTION & FLIGHT of the golf ball. Similar to lesson 2, I suggest that you memorize the terminology and shot patterns that deal with direction. It is important that these descriptions be second nature in your mind in order to avoid getting easily confused.

This lesson is actually more significant than lesson 2 because of all the 'chronic slicers' in the world (statistics say 90%). New golfers, and chronic slicers, need to understand 'why' a golf ball slices and 'how' to make it hook or draw intentionally. They also need to understand that attempting to hit the ball straight (in the early going) is simply wrong, and must be shunned from day one otherwise a multitude of bad habits can set in.

The direction in which a golf ball flies is influenced by spin. The ball is always spinning. Every golf shot you will ever hit will have backspin and sidespin, unless there is no power. The backspin will not be our concern because when the ball is hit solid, the grooves, which are cut into all irons, produce the back spin. Our concern will be the 2 sidespins. The side spin action is made up of two directions: CLOCKWISE and COUNTER CLOCKWISE. Clock wise produces a slice spin and counter clockwise produces a hook spin; STRAIGHT spin can happen purely by chance or through the intentions of an advanced ball striker. At this point, you should work to eliminate the thought of straight, it will only impede your progress.

Golf is similar to various other sports and activities involving an object, where the technique that is used determines how the object flies. In baseball, a pitcher uses a variety of spins to produce curveballs, sinkers and sliders. In tennis a player applies top, bottom and side spins. In billiards players use a variety of sidespins and top and bottom spins as well. Try throwing a frisbee sometime, it slices and hooks just like a golf ball. In golf you only have to worry about clockwise and counter-clockwise spin, the backpin takes care of itself.

Golf's 2 Sidespins

Usable Clockwise spin:
Also known as left to right.

produces pull-fade & pull-slice

Usable Counter clockwise spin:
Also known as right to left.

produces push-draw & push-hook.

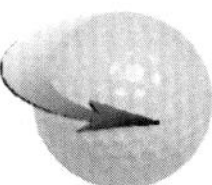

The remainder of lesson 3 will focus on the swing mechanics
which relate to the 4 positive shot patterns

The 4 Negative Shot Patterns

These four shot patterns are unusable.
Be aware of them for evaluation purposes only.

*The pages ahead will guide you toward developing
these four shots patterns.*

For the remainder of this lesson, clockwise & counter clockwise spins will refer only to the usable,

Right to Left

"The better swing you have and the better player you become – as far as hitting the ball that is – the more definitely you become a hooker. The mechanics of a good swing demands a hook." ~ Ben Hogan

Shaping a golf ball from right to left, or hitting draws and hooks is achieved by making the ball spin counter-clockwise. Refer back to pages 62 & 63 to understand the difference between positive counter clockwise spin (CCS) and negative. Positive CCS is referred to as either a push draw or a push hook. This section wants you to develop these two positive ball flights.

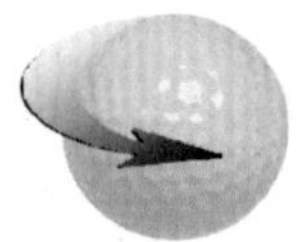

Step 1 ~ The Release

As you are moving the clubhead through the hitting area there is a movement called the release. The release can also be called 'the roll-over' or 'toe up to toe up'. The release happens at the bottom of the swing, approximately 2 feet before the ball to 2 feet after the ball; this is called the hitting area. When entering the hitting area your clubface should be in a fairly open position (figure 1). When moving through this area your clubface should gradually close (figure 2). This open to closed movement is called the release. The release is a very natural and powerful movement to eventually be controlled by the left hand, left wrist, and left forearm (discussed further in lesson 4).

As you are practicing the release by rolling your wrists over, visualize the golf ball spinning when you hit it — keep visualizing the counter clockwise spin.

When hitting full shots, the release will happen so fast it will be a blur. Since many male players can swing the club over 90 miles per hour, it's easy to see why it is a split second event.

counter clockwise spin

Notice in the 'action photo' (figure 3) how my ball is taking off to the right of the target line. This initial take-off is called a PUSH. The bending arrow is showing the ball flight through the air, that being a DRAW. If the ball flight shows a small curve, it is referred to as a draw. If the ball flight shows a big curve it is referred to as a hook (push-draw or push-hook). This particular ball flight is also referred to as RIGHT to LEFT. My ball has started right of the target, then is drawing to the left.

fig 4

fig 5   fig 6

Developing an 'inside-out swing path' combined with the release (or roll over), these 2 major movements are considered the 'one-two punch' in delivering a right to left shot — it is essential that the shot starts to the right of the target then works left with spin (thus right to left).

Here is a basic understanding of the plane (see angle plane line in pictures):

On the backswing (figure 5) a straight take-away will be fine. The backswing should travel more toward the sky (upright), rather than around your body (flat).

On the downswing the hips must always initiate; they will always lead and pull your arms downward. Learn how to loop the club behind you at the start of the downswing, training the arms and hands to be pulled down by the right hip. Your hands might even brush against the right hip pocket (figure 6). Eventually a strong weight shift and hip turn to the left will automatically drop the arms into this position — also known as the slot.

fig 7

fig 8   fig 9

Inside-out is easy to understand when relating the downswing to a clock. The backswing will draw back at 6 o'clock or straight back (figure 5). The downswing must loop the club to the inside as to be attacking the ball from 7 o'clock (figure 4 & 8). The follow-through must continue on this established angle traveling out to 1 o'clock (figure 7 & 9).

This is the inside-out action, a straight take-away, loop the club to the inside on the way down, swing your arms out and away from you on an angle described by 7 o'clock to 1 o'clock (downswing & follow-through only).

This inside-out swing path must then coordinate with the release of the wrists to produce the required counter clockwise spin on the ball, thus delivering a right to left shot. Many people experience difficulty incorporating this move into their swing. Give it a chance and you will be amazed at what it will accomplish!

Step 3 ~ The Strong Grip

Once you have established the 'one-two punch', that being the inside-out swing path combined with the release, the grip then becomes a very important tool for shot making. The strength of your left-hand grip helps to control the clubface during the release (rollover). The strength of your grip is determined by your LEFT-HAND KNUCKLES (not by how tight you hold the club). How many knuckles can you see on your left hand while standing at attention, looking down? If you can see 3 or 4 knuckles this is quite a strong grip (figure 10).

The number of knuckles you show on your left hand will promote more or less club-face closure through the hitting area. For example, if you wanted to hook the ball an extreme amount you would strengthen your grip to 4 knuckles. If you wanted to draw the ball slightly, you might only show 2 knuckles. I strongly encourage you to experiment with different strengths. Show 4 knuckles, 3¹⁄2, 3 knuckles, 2¹⁄2 and so on. By experimenting you are developing an arsenal of weapons to help you overcome the obstacles that are a part of the game — this is shot making!

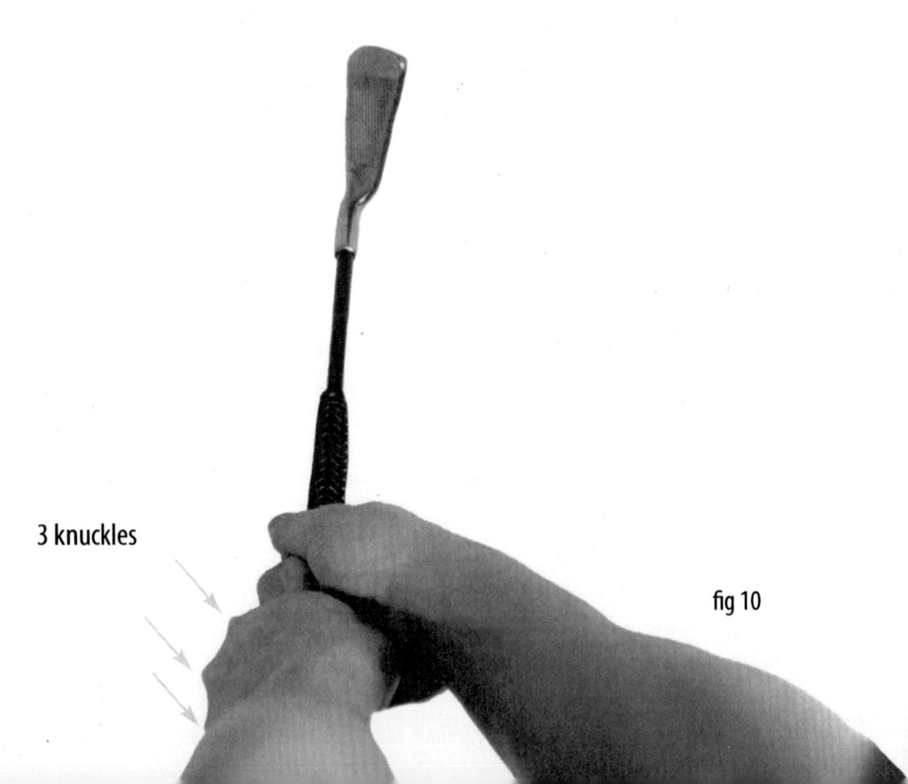

Scan the QR code
to watch a
1 minute
Smash & Carve
demonstration!
SCAN ME
www.smashandcarve.com

Key Thoughts

The right to left shot is simply paramount in becoming a good golfer. With this flight a golfer has, power, predictability, proper trajectory, and a healthy swing. Without this flight a golfer has, not much! It's exactly like Mr. Hogan's quote at the beginning of this section where he says ,"The mechanics of a good swing demands a hook," This statement could not be more true! And he said it more than 50 years ago which is even more interesting as to how the game has not really evolved past him... the legend!

The statistics say that over 90% of all golfers worldwide are considered 'chronic slicers' and a fair percentage of these people are beginners. In studying this fact my entire life it appears that the real culprit to this alarming statistic is the straight shot instead of the right to left shot. If you were to ask a chronic slicer what their swing thoughts are they would say something to this effect, "I take the club back straight, then I try to swing down straight, I then try to swing through the ball straight, and I also try to keep the clubface straight because, that's how I will make the ball go straight." Right? Wrong! Those swing thoughts will slice the ball every time. It might sound logical to an inexperienced golfer but these swing thoughts are terrible. They are actually closer to the 'left to right' swing thoughts you will see in the next section.

In moving forward it is imperative that a golfer 'wants' to develop the right to left shot in their game, you have to like hitting hooks and draws and totally abandon the straight golf shot theory. You know, hooking a golf ball is a very natural, powerful ball flight that relates to various other sports. If you ever watch 10-pin bowling on television, all the players try to hook the bowling ball down the lane. If you ever watch soccer, watch when they hit a corner kick, the ball is always hooking, that's because it is such a natural movement for the body to produce when one gets the hang of it.

Step 4 ~ Alignment

As you are practicing your right to left shots you don't have to aim at anything in particular. I would like you to use the entire right side of the driving range. Your alignment will depend on how excessive you want your hook or draw to be. Just make sure that wherever you aim, the inside out swing path is always promoted.

Short irons are good clubs for practicing hook shape; long irons and woods are more difficult to hook. Practice a variety of curves such as your biggest hook, your smallest hook, and a somewhere in between hook. Aim 5 yards right, 10 yards right, 20, 30 and so on. Also strengthen your grip accordingly; 2 knuckles, 21/2, 3, 31/2, 4. Have some fun experimenting! See if you can just miss the right fence line at your range, then bend the ball with a really large curve back to the left. Practice shaping your ball right to left with a variety of curves. Doing this will add fun to an otherwise tedious practice routine, and will help you to familiarize yourself with your ability to carve the ball. Always remember the two basic shots are draw and hook. The better players in this game can control their shape in 5 yard increments. For example: 5 yard draw, 10, 15, 20 etc. Your shotmaking skills will always be tested during a round of golf; the more control you have over shape the more you will be able to fit a shot to a situation.

Practicing a variety of curves is not only positive for your game but is also a lot of fun. You're allowed to have fun while learning this game of a lifetime. The fun is in the shotmaking!

Left to Right

This section must be understood as far less important to the right to left shot. I have included it to help recreational golfers understand 'why' they slice, and how to work with this flight in the grand scheme. Chronic slicers should focus most of their attention on developing the right to left shot exclusively.

Shaping a golf ball from left to right, or hitting 'fades' and 'slices' is achieved by making the ball spin clockwise. Spinning the ball in this manner can be productive, as long as it's intentional and not by accident.

Step 1 ~ No Release

When understanding the proper release that is required to hit a slice (fade) or a left to right shot, the first thing to realize is that there is no release. It is because of a lack of release that so many players slice the ball — if there is no wrist roll through the hitting area the shot is called 'a block'. The big difference between a hook and a slice is that you roll your wrists to hook (closing the clubface), you don't roll your wrists to slice (clubface stays open, figure 13). As you are practicing this blocking action by not rolling your hands through the hitting area, notice the ball spinning clockwise. The ball will probably go directly to the right because the clubface is still open. When hitting slices the clubface must stay open. When hitting hooks the clubface must close. You either block or release with your hands through the hitting area.

fig 12

fig 13

Clockwise Spin

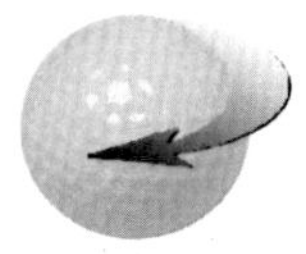

fig 14

Notice in the 'action photo' (figure 14) how my ball is taking off to the left of the target line. This initial take-off is called a PULL. The bending arrow is showing the ball flight through the air, that being a FADE. If the ball flight shows a small curve, it is referred to as a fade. If the ball flight shows a big curve it is referred to as a slice (pull-fade or pull-slice). This particular ball flight is also referred to as LEFT to RIGHT. My ball has started left of the target, then is fading to the right.

fig 15

fig 16   fig 17

An outside-in swing path is a very common swing move shared by many struggling golfers. Considering that most golfers slice, it is a foregone conclusion that most golfers swing from the outside-in. This swing move is considered a flaw for a golfer that can't hit from the inside-out because it's unintentional. If it was intentional, that might be a different story.

Generally a straight takeaway (fig 16) is used. On the downswing, a transition loop opposite of inside-out is made (fig 17). Attacking the ball from 6 o'clock (or straight) is also considered outside the 'angled' plane line.

fig 18

fig 19   fig 20

Outside-in is easy to understand when relating the downswing to a clock. The backswing usually gets drawn back to 6 o'clock or straight back (figure 16). The downswing then loops the club, to the outside, thereby attacking the ball from 5 o'clock (figure 15 &19). Your follow-through will continue on this established angle traveling past the ball to 11 o'clock (figure 18 & 20).

Outside-in is also referred to as 'over the top' and considered by many to be an error. However if this swing move is used intentionally on a limited basis it can add a new dimension to your shotmaking — but only if inside-out becomes your natural move.

Step 3 ~ The Weak Grip

The weakening of your left-hand grip wil help to control the blocking action through impact. Blocking through impact will leave the clubface open, thereby making the golf ball spin clockwise because your wrists won't be able to roll over from this weak grip position. A weak grip will have you standing at attention, looking down, being able to see 1 or 2 knuckles on your left hand (figure 21).

I strongly suggest you experiment with the weakness of your left-hand grip; you should be able to show a 1 knuckle grip and a 2 knuckle grip. These two grips relate to the 2 basic shots on this side of the ball: the fade and the slice, or left to right.

The weak grip may not be as important as the strong grip because so many golfers already have trouble with slicing. Periodically practicing the slice, or the fade, is still healthy practice and will not pose a problem as long as you understand the fundamentals that control the shot.

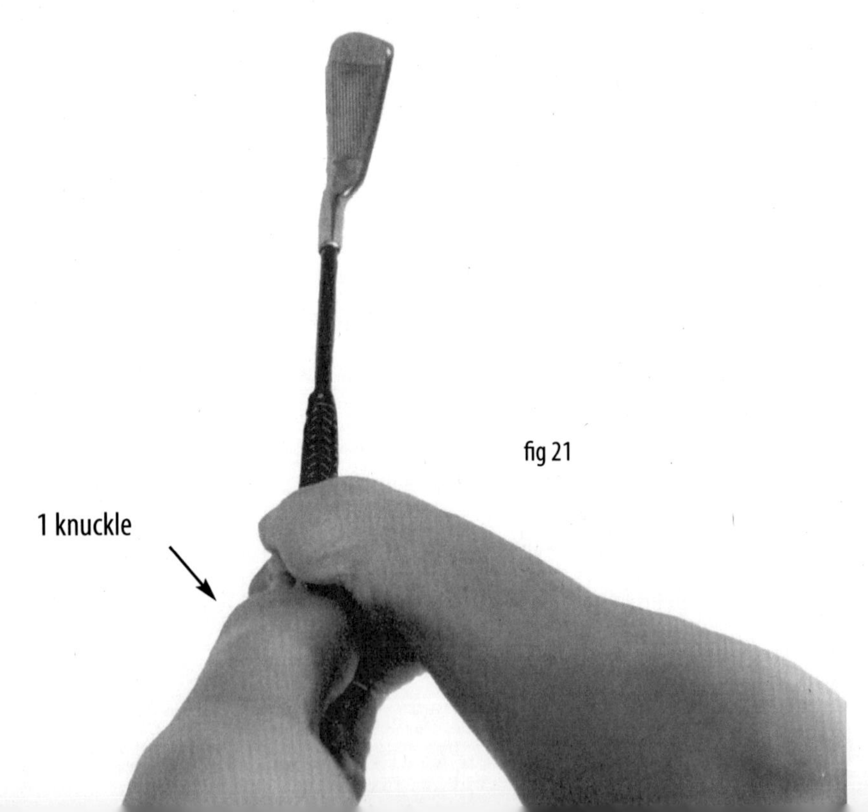

Scan the QR code
to watch a
1 minute
Smash & Carve
demonstration!

SCAN ME

www.smashandcarve.com

Step 4 ~ Alignment

As you are practicing these left to right shots using the weaker left-hand grip, combined with an outside-in swing path (or your regular swing path), you don't have to aim at anything in particular. I would like you to use the entire left side of the driving range, as opposed to the right side we were using to practice the right to left shot. Your alignment will depend on the club you choose and how excessive you want the slice or fade to be. A good club selection for practicing your slice shape would be a 5-iron. When practicing your left to right shape it is okay to go down in club selection because the shot will tend to go much higher than right to left. Hooks will generally fly quite low and slices tend to fly much higher (do you understand why?). Practice a variety of curves, starting with the biggest slice you have. See if you can just miss the left fence line at your range, then bend the ball back to the right. Practice big and small left to right shape using the fundamentals put forth in this section and aiming varying degrees to the left. However, be careful with this shot as you could just aim left and, by using your normal swing, have the ball slice all by itself. In general, most golfers should almost exclusively practice the right to left shot.

fig 22

Summary

In conclusion to this lesson on direction and the swing mechanics that control the flight of the ball, remember that golf is a shotmaker's game and your ability to control the direction 'with shape' will keep your game constantly improving over time. Of course, the ultimate goal is to be able to shape the ball both ways using the four basic shots which are, draw, hook, fade and slice. These curves/flights are achieved by understanding how clockwise and counter-clockwise spin effects the ball flight, and how certain swing movements promote these two opposite spins.

As I continue to understand the characteristics of the recreational golfer, it has become very clear to me that the hook/draw spin (counter-clockwise) needs to be promoted and encouraged on a grand scale. Unfortunately it is not being promoted and taught nearly enough, which is why there are 'as many' chronic slicers in the world today as there were 20, 30 & 50 years ago. Isn't that rather bizarre? With all this supposed new technology? Anybody can hook and draw the ball if they really want to.

Keep trying to become a 'chronic hooker' instead of a chronic slicer! Get your game well away from that alarming statistic that says 90% of all golfers are chronic slicers. If slicing is the only shot you have in your bag, and it's unintentional, you will never experience the true pleasures of the game, and your game will always be considered weak, on many different levels. Also, the further in time you go as a chronic slicer the more difficult it will be to convert you over to the other side? You know, as a reward, hooking the ball goes much further than slicing!

In closing, be smart in your development. Learning how to shape the ball from right to left is initially quite difficult and needs some time to be made natural. While you are learning, if you are having trouble hitting draws and hooks on the course, play your slice or fade when it really matters. Work on the weak parts of your game until they are strong enough to play on the course.

lesson 4

SUPINATION:RELEASE

The impact area in golf or — IMPACT — as it is often referred, is without a doubt the most exciting and dynamic part of the swing. This area has the ability to make a good looking swing perform badly, or a bad looking swing perform well. This area must be held at the forefront of all swing fundamentals. There have been many good and great golfers over the years who constantly say, "Impact is everything"! This statement only reinforces the 'ball-to-swing-learning theory' I am such a big fan of. To my knowledge, Ben Hogan brought attention to the impact area unlike any player/teacher before, or after, his 1957 book, Five Lessons. Great players from all over the globe are still studying what he did, and what he had to say... myself included.

TV golf analyst (CBS), Peter Kostis, referred to Ben Hogan as the, 'Inventor of Supination', through impact, and also the, 'inventor of the swing plane'. That's pretty impressive! These next two chapters will be an understanding into these two critical areas in golf and how they relate to both a recreational and advanced golfer.

Supination, or the release as it is often referred to today, takes place through the hitting area. It happens approximately 2 feet before the ball, to 2 feet past the ball and is 'a motion', not a position. The release has already been discussed in some detail back in chapter 3 (right to left shots, page 65) and if most golfers would simply learn this all-important flight, much of the proper release in the swing would naturally develop.

This chapter will expand on how left-hand supination through impact greatly affects the performance areas in the swing. those areas being contact & direction (smash & carve). As you will see in the upcoming pages, supination plays a two-part role through the hitting area; it helps to 'deloft' the club (contact supination) and it also helps to 'draw the ball' by controlling the rollover (directional supination). This is why referring to the impact area as 'left-hand supination' is far superior than 'the release', but throughout this chapter I will refer to both from time to time.

Supination (the release) happens at impact and beyond (figures 2, 3 and 4), and refers to the function of the left hand, left wrist, and left forearm only. In order to practice this significant action effectively, a dominant weight shift to the left foot along with an inside out swing path is mandatory. The proper release is called supination. It's a rollover through impact with your left wrist (for a right-handed golfer) leading the clubhead.

fig 1

fig 2

Practicing Draws & Hooks is excellent for developing supination - direction (p. 69)

fig 3   fig 4

The function of the right hand and right arm will not be discussed at all during this lesson, the reason being that the right hand and arm must always follow the leading left. Even though my right hand appears to overtake my left in figure 4, I am actually focused only on keeping my left wrist and arm leading. The right (bottom hand) is so powerful it never needs to be exercised or stressed through impact. If and when the right is dominating, poor results are sure to follow.

Pronation vs Supination

DEFINITIONS FROM WEBSTER'S ILLUSTRATED DICTIONARY

Pronation: To turn the palm of the hand (or inner surface of a forelimb) downward or backward.

In golf this movement is needed during the backswing and downswing. Essentially, pre-impact involves left-hand pronation.

Supination: To turn the palm and forearm upward.

In golf this movement is needed at impact and beyond. Essentially, post-impact involves left-hand supination.

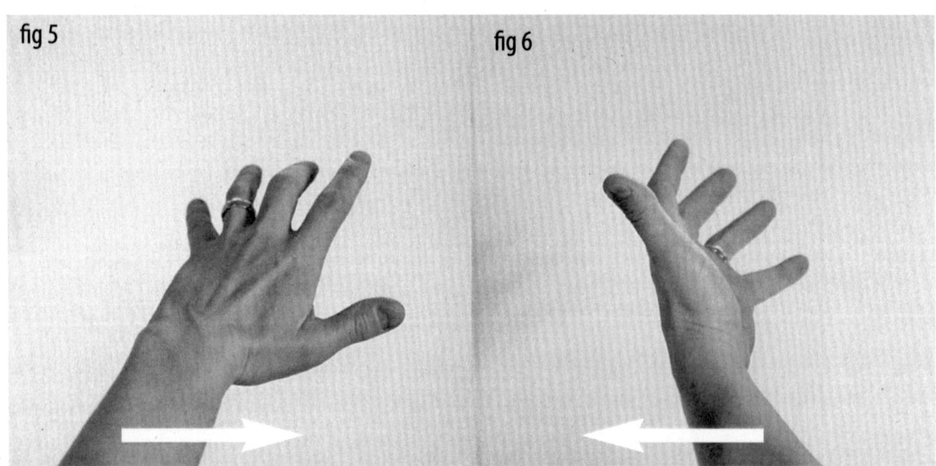

I strongly encourage you to practice this left-handed movement without a club as much as possible. Air swings can be practiced anytime and will build coordination, memory and strength into the preferable dominant side.

Practicing with your right hand and right arm is not necessary because the left must always control the right. Start strengthening your left side as soon as possible.

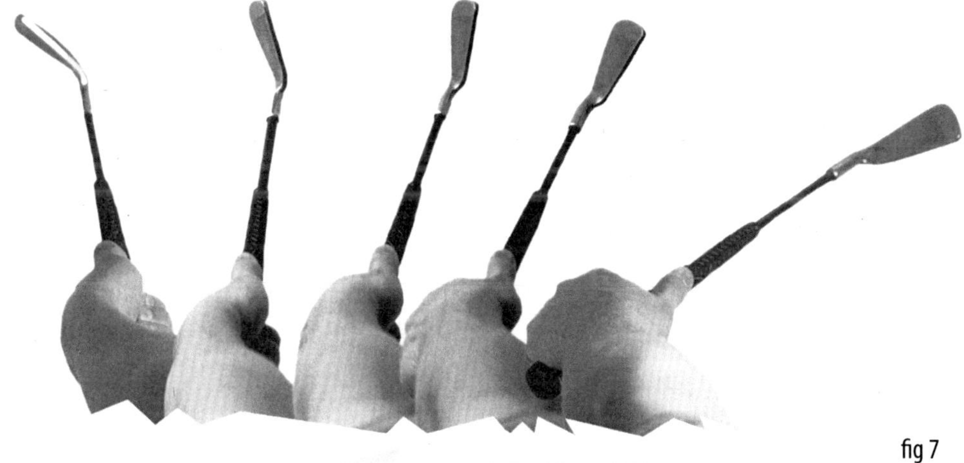

fig 7

When swinging a golf club, the transition from pronation to supination (the release) can happen quickly or slowly depending on how much power is applied. This action happens just-before-impact-till-just-after-impact. The tighter this movement surrounds the ball the better.

Supination is two-fold. To understand it fully we have to break it down into two separate areas: directional supination and contact supination.

Directional Supination

Please refer to figure 7 and notice how the left hand rolls the clubface over through the hitting area, showing the palm of the left hand to the player. This is directional supination. Initially this movement was discussed in lesson 3 (right to left golf shots). The 'left-hand release' is also known as directional supination and when combined with the strength of the left hand knuckles, the more the clubface will close during the hitting area. If the left hand supination through impact is too great, creating too much hook, then weakening the left-hand knuckles is required. Chances are this will not be the case if you take into consideration that so many golfers slice the ball. Supination is a standard, you must work with it, not against it, on all shots. Slicers try to keep the club-face straight or square, steering through impact rather than developing and trusting the 'roll-over action' These are two very different schools of thought. In order to experience the natural power of release you must let go of the notion that the clubface stays straight through impact. The only sure way to effectively control the clubface is through left-hand supination.

Contact Supination

During the roll-over action as shown in figure 7 (previous page) the left wrist must also 'bow' or lean forward through impact. This bending of the left wrist toward the target will deloft the clubface and allow the palm of the left hand to be seen by the player (fig 8). This is contact supination.

fig 8   fig 9

While this 'magical move' freaks out the newly converted, the longer you can 'flow the left wrist' into this bowed position the better (all the way to the 1/2 or even the 3/4 follow through position). Eventually, with practice, the results are absolutely astounding. Don't be afraid to exaggerate this move.

This movement was previously discussed in lesson 2 (Contact). If the hands are leading the clubhead through the hitting area, supination will be achieved (figure 8). Bowing the left wrist toward the target will contribute strongly to that all-important divot, which is taken after the ball (refer to page 40 & 41).

Eventually contact supination and directional Supination will need to be combined to create one fluid movement. When this left-handed action becomes a comfortable part of the swing, a player has tremendous potential to excel.

When done correctly, this two-fold movement should produce a low hook (counter-clockwise spin) indicating a healthy and workable foundation to build on.

Negative Pronation

Also known as scooping, left-hand pronation through impact (figure 11) is the opposite of the correct supinating action. When the clubhead passes the hands, the 'cupped' or scooped left wrist will be facing up making it impossible to hit the ball solid because the club will be on its way up rather than down through impact (fig 9).

fig 10   fig 11

During the swing motion, left-hand pronation is needed in the backswing and downswing only. It is not until impact that the left hand will make the transition to supination (refer to figure 7). If the left hand continues to pronate (or scoop) through impact (figure 10), power will be lost and a multitude of errors can take place.

- Don't be a scooper!
- Don't let the clubhead pass your hands!
- Don't keep the clubface straight of square.
- Don't try to 'get under it'.

> *Advanced Player Note: Low handicap players and professionals, for the most part, have developed away from supination, it just happens for them automatically. They say simple things like, 'Hold the angle through the ball and hit down', (page 55 fig 27 & 28), and 'Let it release' or 'Hold it off' to shape the ball (lesson 3 Direction).*

Summary

The releasing action through impact is best referred to as 'left-hand supination'. This 2-part move combines together in a good swing to help achieve consistent contact and predictable direction. Smash & Carve is contact and direction.

The culprit (bad habit maker) through impact seems to be the 'straight shot golf theory'. When a golfer applies this wrong theory it is impossible to develop proper divot taking because the left wrist wants to pronate/scoop through impact as the golfer is attempting to keep the blade straight (Fig. 10 & 11). By trying to keep the blade straight the left wrist pronates — this is bad news!

This wrong 'straight theory' also plays a major role in the statistic that states 90% of golfers are slicers. Chronic slicers become that way because of the straight shot theory. By trying to keep the clubface straight during impact the golfer doesn't realize that the clubface is technically open, and not square as they might think. Instead of the clubface gradually closing (Fig.7) the openness of the blade is the initial reason as to 'why' golfers slice, and it is drawn back to the made-up straight theory.

The base shot to work from is the push-hook! (see the front cover!). Also known as right to left, this basic shot exudes excellence, and will take care of much of the proper release through impact. You want to develop a push-draw/hook on a fairly low trajectory. This flight combines both contact supination and directional supination. When this flight is easy for you to produce regularly, straight shots are then possible, and so is carving the ball from left to right.

lesson 5

Engine Moves

One of the greatest things about golf is that it doesn't require size, speed or strength to be a really good player; although these attributes are what most other sports are built upon. This is why I have always liked comparing learning golf to learning to play a musical instrument, because these instruments like golf, require varying degrees of technical difficulty in order to continue playing at advanced levels. Good golf, especially great golf, requires correct knowledge. If a player has the knowledge, and applies it over an extended period of time with practice, like learning music, the player will excel.

This lesson will expand on the advanced movements in the golf swing or 'The Engine Moves'. These moves/fundamentals are: The Plane, The Slot, and The Release all triggered by the action of the hips. I find it fascinating when I watch high level golf and see the many different body types and athletic abilities, combined with many different looking golf swings. They can all hit the ball so well but no two swings are exactly alike, that is until one watches and analyzes their swings on video. This is where you have the luxury of slow motion playback to see how well the 'Engine Moves' in their swings relate to the ideal theory and to the great players of the past.

Keep in mind while studying this lesson there will always be exceptions to these fundamental rules I am promoting. Because golf is such an individual game there are many different techniques that can show excellent results for a period of time, however these results can diminish over time as a player gets older or nerves start to appear. This is when a player needs to start rebuilding their swing. As a technique that was once reliable begins to fall apart.

Lesson five is based on researched information substantiated by past and present tour players. Anyone who has played golf for a long time and considers themselves a good player should find this lesson very helpful in understanding the makings of a great golf swing, and will hopefully assist in bringing their game to a higher level.

Ben Hogan's Vision

I would like to start this lesson with a concept put forth from the great Ben Hogan way back in 1957 (fig. 1). It comes from his book Five Lessons ~ The Modern Fundamentals of Golf. Until recently (2008), I never truly realized just how significantly this fundamental affected the swing plane, the slot area and the impact zone because of 'where' it was located in his book, and how little it was promoted by Mr Hogan throughout. Observing my peers and the best players on the tour it is obvious to me how many of them endorse this theory (of keeping the arms close together) especially in the slot area and through impact, which leads me back to Mr Hogan's book. The illustration below clearly illustrates this concept.

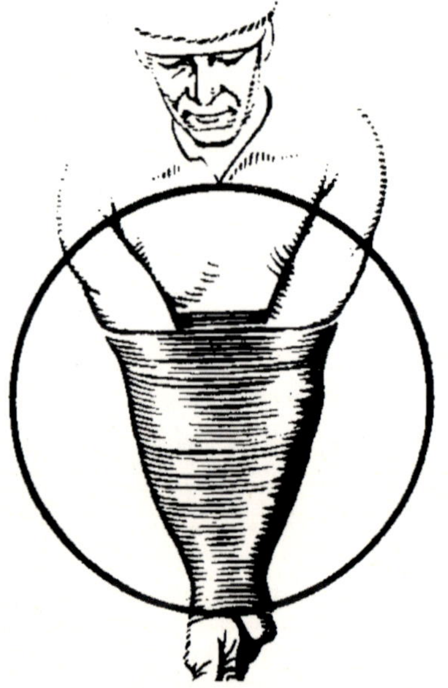

fig 1

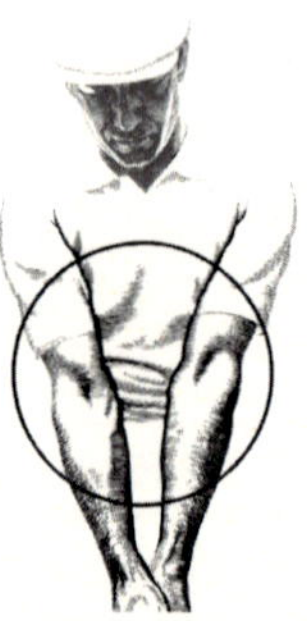

Keep the elbows and arms as close together as possible throughout the entire swing.

Ben Hogan ~ 1957

Say Hello To My Little Friend!

I made myself a swing trainer that encompasses the concept Mr Hogan had in mind, and follows the common thread that you will see in most of the touring professionals on television from week to week. 'The Klamp' (my nickname for it), is a comfortable swing trainer made out of 'no flex' materials, with a joiner in between. You can buy variations of this online or just use a belt, or anything to secure your arms together while grooving the feel.

fig 2

fig 3

When using The Klamp the purpose is to keep the arms from separating at the top of the backswing and, more importantly, in the slot and through impact. Training aids are useful, but in my opinion the best ones allow you to actually hit balls while using them, rather than just trying to develop a 'feel' in the swing motion. When you actually hit balls the body often wants to do different things than it does with air swings.

(Note: most training aids are safe to use while hitting balls, but it's advisable initially not to hit 100% effort shots. Work up to that.)

The Backswing Plane

The understanding of the swing plane begins with an 'angled line' running from the golf ball, through the bottom of the golfer's neck (Figs 4 to 11).

On the backswing, while keeping the arms as close together as possible (with or without The Klamp) the general idea is to swing your arms back, and up, trying to keep your hands and the angle of your 'straight left arm' as close to the plane line as possible. You will notice my hands and left arm stay underneath the plane line during the entire backswing (figs 5, 6, 7): this is a good thing. If the hands and arms get above the plane line at any time during the backswing, this is not recommended, and is commonly referred to as 'outside' or too upright.

fig 4   fig 5

At the top of the backswing (fig. 7) you will notice that my hands and left arm are noticeably underneath the plane line. If my hands get too far below this line at the top, it is referred to as too flat a backswing. If my hands and left arm end up above the plane line at the top, it is referred to as too upright a backswing. Ideally at the top of the backswing, you want your hands and left arm to be as close to this plane line as possible, without venturing above the angled plane line.

For the backswing to be considered excellent, the other areas involved are, the flatness of the left wrist versus cupping or bowing, and the direction the clubshaft points (left, right or down the line). In keeping these areas short and concise, it would be very good to have the left wrist flat at the top, and the club shaft pointing down the target line. You will notice my left wrist is flat, and my club shaft points a little to the left of my target line (fig. 7). This is not a bad thing by any means. Pointing the clubshaft to the left or down the target line is desired by better players.

fig 6   fig 7

When working on your backswing plane it is essential that a golfer has access to either a mirror or some form of video, like a cell phone camera. Due to the fact that you can't see your plane angle when you are hitting balls it becomes imperative that one does a lot of practice backswings using a mirror (at least) with the angled plane line drawn on the mirror (use a 'non-permanent' felt pen). Usually a driving range has a mirror handy somewhere for keen golfers to use. Videos are the best because they show your swing 'in action'. That is why videos are the most helpful training tool for golf because they won't let your swing lie, like practice swings can do. Most golfers have some kind of access to video, like the cameras on smart phones. They work well and are so easy to use! Just sit your phone on your golf bag at the range (or get a tripod) and start treating your swing like the hobby that it is. You can watch it on the spot or archive your swing in your computer — it's very easy, and it's the most powerful tool a golfer can use when working on their golf swing. It's also interesting and fun!

The Downswing Plane

The downswing should always begin with something from the lower body. You either turn your hips to the left, or fire your right knee into the shot ahead of your arms. Clear the hips is the best swing thought to begin the downswing. As you will see in fig. 9 my right heel is already partially up off the ground showing a driving action from my lower body. This is where the video camera is again very helpful to see exactly how much lower body action you are using in your downswing. A standard rule of thumb is that if you end up being flat footed at impact you are not using enough lower body action.

fig 8   fig 9

In understanding the downswing plane relative to the angled plane line, pay attention to where my hands and left arm go in the transition from backswing to the slot area (figs 8 & 9). Notice how my hands and left arm are noticeably underneath the plane line, or inside (fig. 9). As suggested back in lesson three (pages 66 & 67) a 'transition loop' where the club appears to be hitting the ball from 7 o'clock is a good initial understanding of this all-important transition from backswing to slot area.

If your hands and left arm are not noticeably under the plane line, it is not inside enough. If your hands and left arm venture above the plane line at any time on the downswing, this is not good and will always lead to chronic slicing, or pulled shots to the left.

Hitting the golf ball from the 'inside' is considered a major goal in the game because the hands can learn and adopt the same message from this inside attack angle, that being to release or roll over. The clearing of the hips, combined with this inside attack angle are both very relative to controlling the proper wrist action through the ball. The wrist action during the release plays such an important role to high quality golf, and the inside attack angle has a tremendous influence on this 'rollover action' through impact, but only if the hips have cleared properly. Mr Hogan used to call this downswing sequence the chain action and if done properly the player will most definitely become a hooker of the golf ball! Please refer back to lesson 3 (right to left shots, page 65).

fig 10   fig 11

Advanced 'downswing plane' thoughts

In an ideal sense if you can imagine, you would want both arms very close together at the top of the backswing, then both arms still very close together in the slot area, as both arms and both hands try to stay close to the leading hips (fig. 9 & 10). This is the true meaning of inside. It means both arms and both hands are very close to the clearing hip spin coming down and into the hitting area. When I experiment with the Smash & Carve Klamp (fig. 2) it assures me that my arms are staying together, then I can try to get the entire unit (hands and arms) brushing very close to my body and just missing my right thigh through the slot area.

Vertical arm position

When the downswing plane is done exceptionally well and the arms are staying very close together, there is a distinct look slightly before impact where both arms are almost vertical (fig. 10). My positions in figs 9 & 10 are not bad but, I continue to work at the togetherness of both arms, and both arms grazing the body on the way down which will give me that 'vertical right arm' position, in the slot and slightly before impact, that I see in the great players.

The Klamp

When I use my trainer (The Klamp) and then I compare certain areas in my own swing (with and without it on), the high quality positions I achieve are simply astounding! This is one reason why doing this new chapter is so exciting for me because I am able to compare my new swing (2010) to my old swing pictures in the previous chapters to which go back to approximately 1998. The three main areas in the swing that The Klamp helps improve are: The backswing, the slot area, and the impact zone.

The Backswing: When you compare my new backswing position (fig. 12) versus my old backswing position (fig. 13) you will notice a big difference where my right elbow is located. My old backswing has a noticeable 'flying' right elbow compared with a much tighter and connected position in the new backswing. They say the ideal right elbow position will be pointing almost straight down and in fig. 12 while wearing The Klamp it is just that.

The Slot: My new slot area (fig. 14) keeps my right elbow much more in front of my body instead of drifting behind my body in the old slot area (fig. 15). In the old slot area you will notice my left arm beginning to bend and soften, this is not good. In the new slot area you will see my left arm stays straight, and solid. One of the really interesting things I have found while using The Klamp is that it has solved the 'bent left arm theory' that many players have. Through experimentation, it appears that if a player has a bent left arm in the slot, or at impact, it is because of the separation of the arms in the downswing.

Impact: My new impact area (fig. 16) is very good now, and compares to the many great golf swings of the past and present. The closer the arms can stay together on the backswing and downswing will ensure a dynamic impact position and also a straight left arm. As you can see in my old impact position (fig. 17) my left arm is partially bent, and soft, because of the separation of the arms that started from my flying right elbow in my backswing.

Since about 2005 I have been going through a rebuilding process in my own game and was searching for answers to certain questions, these questions were mainly to do with the slot area, the impact zone, and the release. I believe that I have found all the answers to my questions through the help of The Klamp Swing Trainer, and with my video camera. I hope after you read through this lesson, some of your long time questions will get answered too.

2010 backswing position (fig. 12)

1998 backswing position (fig. 13)

2010 Slot position (fig. 14)

1998 Slot position (fig. 15)

2010 Impact position (fig. 16)

1998 Impact position (fig. 17)

The Slot

fig. 18

fig. 19

fig. 20

A better player will often refer to the golf swing in this manner. "I take it up, drop it in the slot, then I let 'er go." It sounds simple enough but the knowledge and years of practice trying to achieve these advanced areas has to be appreciated.

The downswing plane works in tandem with the 'delaying action' to help achieve the ultimate slot area (figs 19 & 20). The slot would be considered by many to be the most important area in the golf swing, and cannot be properly accessed without the proper clearing of the hips on the downswing.

Here are some keys to help achieve a dynamic slot area in your swing:

First: Work with video regularly (use your phone).

Second: Clear the hips to start the downswing.

Third: Keep the arms tight together. Ideally (in fig. 20) I would like to see my arms much closer together.

Fourth: Hit from the inside. The understanding of the downswing plane and how close the arms need to be together in conjunction with the closeness your arms and hands get to your right thigh (fig 20).

Fifth: Maintain the wrist hinge. Another famous quote from Ben Hogan is, "I just bring my backswing position down". Which means, you should be trying to maintain as much wrist hinge as possible right down to the ball.

If you have never worked on your slot area, you will have to do so in practice swings initially. Then, when you start hitting balls, you should do so very soft at first, maybe only 20 or 30 yard shots. Changing your swing is difficult and takes time. If you always hit the ball hard, and never do any slow motion type practice swings, changing your swing will never happen.

They say that a picture is worth a thousand words, and if that's the case then this action photo of Mr Hogan is worth all of them. He used to call the slot area (fig. 21, first position) 'the ready position'. I want you to pay particular attention to the location of his right elbow and notice how it is very close, if not attached to his right hip. If you can imagine using something similar to my 'Klamp' swing trainer to help keep the arms very close together, then on the downswing trying to achieve this similar position by brushing your arms and hands against your body, this will achieve that vertical arm position before impact seen in the best players. Both arms also become significantly inside the plane, to which are both major goals in a good golf swing. Hogan's slot position (shown in this photo) is such a great example of sound mechanics it allows me to fully understand the ultimate goal of the golf swing — to work like a machine. His hips are leading, arms very close together, right elbow brushes against the body, wrists still cocked, the ultimate ready position!

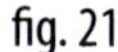
fig. 21

The Release

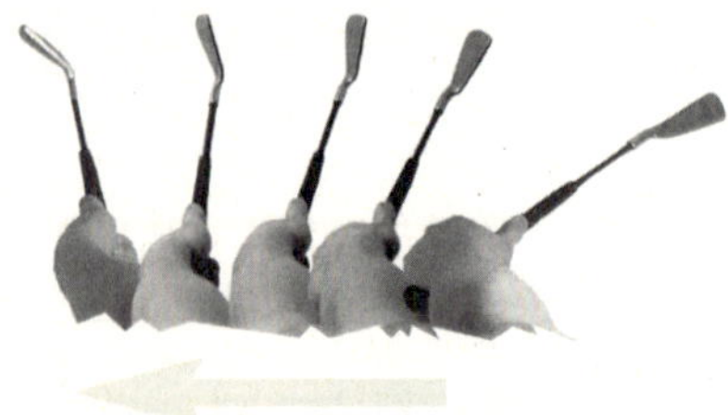

fig. 22

fig. 23

fig. 24

The release, or left hand supination was discussed in much detail during lesson four. The proper release cannot happen without the proper dominance and clearing of the hips on the down-swing. Speaking from many years of trial and error, if the hips do not clear properly it becomes physically impossible to develop a trustworthy release!

The reason why most golfers should promote a left-wrist rollover (supination) is because of their total dominance from their right hand and right arm on the downswing. The goal of the release is to have the rollover dominated by the left wrist, but this can only happen if the left hand-wirst has been educated and strengthened. The best exercise is to swing the club with just your left hand in a small manner, then also try to hit some balls with just your left hand. In time you will increase the strength in this all-important hand and wrist.

Low handicap players and professionals do not try to release, they simply hold the wrist delay through the ball and 'let it release' when they want (fig 27 & 26).

The grip relative to the release

The rollover action you see in fig. 22 is being done with a neutral grip position. If I was to use a stronger grip (page 68) it would promote the clubface to close more through the ball, thus delivering more of a draw ball flight. If I were to use a weaker grip (page 76) it would promote the clubface to stay more open through the ball, thus delivering more of a fade ball flight. The supinating/release action of the left hand will stay constant, but the clubface will react to the relative strength or weakness of the grip at set-up.

The Late Release

fig. 25

fig. 26

fig. 27

Without a doubt the late release in the golf swing is the toughest and most advanced move there is. All good players have it, but it is very difficult to learn, and it is very difficult to teach.

Throughout the previous chapters we have indirectly, been talking about a late release. In lesson two ~ Contact we talked about the emphasis to hit the ball on a lower trajectory, this thought in itself will promote a later release point by trying to deloft the clubface. In lesson three ~ Direction we talked about the importance of being a hooker, and not a slicer, this in itself will promote a release, or a roll over. So, that means when one tries to hit a low draw, or a low hook on every shot, good things are being promoted in the swing action to help develop this all-important 'late release' that all good players have.

So we know the release is a roll-over (fig. 22), so now, how do we do it later? If the roll-over happens before the ball, this is called an early release. If the roll-over happens after the ball, this is a late release. Remember, all good and great players have a very late release, that's one reason why they hit the ball so far!

The downswing sequence works like this: the hips clear with very little sliding. The arms then hit well from the inside. The wrists then maintain their wrist hinge for as long as possible (this is the late in late release Fig 27). The release then happens almost without trying, but only if the hips have cleared properly and the arm swing has hit the ball enough from the inside.

Quite frankly, some moves in the golf swing are very difficult and do take many years to develop, and the ultimate late release is one of them. Even if you know what to do and you have video tools to help, some moves just take a long time, especially if one is trying to become world class.

The Engine

The proper downswing sequence is where really good golf can develop. Without the proper sequential movements a player might end up working hard with no results to show.

When learning the proper downswing sequence though, most players will not be able to have everything right away, these moves do take time to develop. The proper release takes time to learn, the proper inside attack angle takes time, the proper hip action takes time. It all takes time, perhaps many years, and the order one learns these engine moves might be different from the next person.

When you combine this 'clearing of the hips' with the 'inside attack angle' (arms together) you end up with a very interesting perspective. The hips spin left and the arms goes right. This is the centrifugal force action of the engine move, or the 'chain action'.

The Big Picture

Throughout this lesson we have been promoting the advanced moves in the golf swing, or as I like to call them — The Engine Moves! These fundamental movements like the rest of this book are attempting to unite the two major goals, those being contact & direction or Smash & Carve.

The theme of Smash & Carve golf is timeless, it has been around forever! If you let your mind drift for a minute and think back to the early days of the British Open, way back say in about 1868 when Old Tom Morris Sr. was the king of that era, don't you think he was Smashin' & Carvin'? Or what about in the early 1900's when Harry Vardon was the king of that era, don't you think he was Smashin' & Carvin'? Or how about in the 40's, & 50's when my idol Ben Hogan was the king, don't you think he was Smashin' & Carvin' too? Of course he was! And so was Nicklaus, Palmer, Lopez, Watson, Sorenstam, Tiger, Phil and whoever else I can think of.

S M A S H   **C A R V E**

Smash & Carve were the facts to good golf over 100 years ago and they will continue to be the facts 100 years from now, that's because the theme is indisputable! Now if a debate is required to decide the best way to go about achieving these almighty swing goals, then so be it. There are certainly different ways, and different swing moves to go about achieving Smash & Carve that might be different than the moves I am promoting.

Summary

Throughout this lesson the Engine Moves in the golf swing have been discussed and promoted in detail but, wouldn't you like to hear what all the tour players had to say about these moves? I sure would, in detail, but they never seem to divulge much information do they? It's almost like their important swing mechanics are a big secret or something. I don't know about you but I'm getting really tired of hearing the same old cliches like: 'I just focus on my tempo', or 'I'm really trying to zoom in on my target', or, 'Balance, I'm trying to swing in balance and stick my finish'. You know what I'm talking about with these guys and gals? They either think we are all idiots, or they don't want to tell us what they are doing? Could they not give us something to chew on for goodness sake! Do any of them talk about how they set the club at the top? Do any of them talk about their move down? Any talk of the slot, the plane, the release — nothing!

I once heard Tiger Woods say in an interview after a round that he, "Couldn't hit a draw today".

I thought, "Finally"! But guess what, Tiger didn't expand at all on 'why' he couldn't hit a draw on that day, nor did he talk about 'what' he was going to go work on? It's very frustrating.

If I had it my way, I would love to have 20 or 30 tour pros available to ask these questions: "How do you set the club at the top and why?" "How do you start the downswing?" "What are your thoughts on the plane?" "What are your thoughts on the slot area?" and "How do you release the club?" This would be an excellent question and answer period and much would be learned about who are the most conventional and mechanical swingers of the club versus who are strictly feel players and less mechanical. Every good golfer does work with the 'mechanics' in some form or another but quite often many of them find intimate/different ways that work for them. Good golf is a combination of natural ability with some, or all of the proper mechanics.

After teaching and playing at a high level for many years, unlike most advanced players, I'm going to explain exactly what my swing thoughts are on every golf shot I play, in practice and in a game. Some of these swing thoughts I have used for many years and some are quite new:

1. I always look down at my grip and set it accordingly for the shot I will be hitting. Stronger for a draw, weaker for a fade, or more neutral for relatively straight.

2. On the backswing my main thoughts are to keep my arms very close together (I practice a lot with The Klamp) and I always work to make my backswing more upright, because it tends to get too flat.

3. On the downswing is where the bulk of the work comes in. The main moves I work with are to clear the hips, then look like I am looping the club from backswing to downswing, so I am hitting the ball enough from the inside.

This is why I have to make my backswing more upright without going above the plane line because it gives me more room to transition the downswing to the inside. This looping action is not only good for the recreational player, but is also beneficial for a good player. I then try and do this same looping action wearing The Klamp, which makes things much more difficult but, through the help of video, I see the many benefits in my dynamics. (It should be noted that my main shot pattern while practicing is mainly a push-draw. I'll hit 80% push-draws, 15% non-draws, and 5% fades). In conjunction with the looping action and while wearing The Klamp periodically, I try to focus on that picture of Hogan (fig. 21 left picture). I work on keeping my arms well to the inside coming down, combined with maintaining the wrist cock past the ball (fig. 27).

4. At the bottom of the swing I try to hold the wrist angle through impact and let it release on its own. I will pay close attention to my trajectory. I would rather be a low ball hitter because it makes my release feel better through impact.

In short: my swing thoughts would sound like this: Keep the arms tight together at the top, clear the hips to start the downswing, arms tight to the body, right elbow past right hip to release late. These are my practice swing thoughts and quite often good players swing thoughts can sound a little complicated.

My actual game thoughts: get a little simpler but not by much, they would be: Arms close together at the top, clear the hips, hit from the inside. So there you go, my intimate swing thoughts for the record.

Without a doubt golf can be a very complicated game which is why it requires many years to become a truly good or great player. When you are a keen practicer, and have done so for many years, perhaps only one of these swing thoughts I have put forth here in this lesson might prove to be invaluable to you and your game. I, personally, have always wanted to know the whole puzzle and how each piece fits together. Like I said earlier, wouldn't it be great to get inside tour player's heads and pick their brains about their intimate swing thoughts, not only with their game in the present but how they developed as junior golfers and the many breakthroughs they had along the way. It would be fascinating to say the least!

Practice With A Purpose

Do you love practicing? I sure do! I have always enjoyed finding places to practice within a big city like Vancouver. I love discovering that cool spot where I can take my shag balls, whether its the beach, the airport, or any open space where I am all alone to do what I love to do — hit balls! I try to tell this to my students all the time. "Get yourself a bag of balls, go here, go there, search for turf. It's great for your game and it's free!" You don't have to be at a golf course to practice, you just need a bag of practice balls.

So you have your own practice balls now, and you've found a place to hit them, great! So what's the goal? I'll always remember this quote from my junior days. "He hit a bag of seven irons and you could have thrown a blanket over them." Exaggerated perhaps, but a tight spread is the goal. Let's say your practice bag has fifty balls in it, and you're going to hit them all with a nine iron, your goal would be to have all fifty balls end up very close together. If you find that your spread is quite erratic and your balls are flying all over the place, then you're trying to hit them too far. Don't start too big, start small: 60 yards, then 100 yards, etc. How tight is your spread? Show control.

Practicing at a driving range is not the best environment for improving your game, even though it can be convenient. You can usually park your car very close, you don't have to pick up any balls, and you can practice under cover when it's raining or, at night, under the lights. These are the positives and they have a lot of merit, especially in today's high paced lifestyle. The negatives, however, present a challenge for your improvement. For example, at a driving range, you are not able to see your 'spread'. Even the word DRIVING range implies power. Use the driver, hit it as far and as crooked as you can. Control? Who needs control? Somebody else picks them up. When it comes to comparing mats versus turf or sand, because of the high cost of maintaining the turf at a driving range, it has become increasingly rare to find a range with grass to hit off. Mats are the norm, especially in colder climates. We practice off a mat yet we play off grass, talk about different! Hitting off a mat cannot provide you with the all important divot pattern. Mats also instill a false sense of security because the clubhead bounces into the ball when you hit it 'fat' allowing you to believe that your contact is great until you get out to play. Hitting off grass or sand will not build false illusions into your game. Also, because of the wood or cement base that is underneath the mat, you can hurt yourself through repeated impact— I did.

Practice with a purpose — hopefully this doesn't sound too regimented. This is not meant to imply that you can't have fun, just be aware that the purpose of practice is to build consistency. The concepts put forth in Smash and Carve are there for that very reason. But this can only happen if you practice with some regularity. The more you practice the luckier you'll get. If you don't practice, who knows? It will be a guessing game from day to day. There will never be a replacement for hard work, which makes me laugh a little when I think about golf club technology.

This driver hits it further, this club spins more, this putter sinks more; it's all fine equipment but it will never provide you with a truly sound game. Manufacturers have gotten to the point where they are going backwards. Now the popular slogan is, 'oversize is over-rated!' This, after most players own oversize drivers. Where does it end? The simple truth is, a good player can play well with anything, it doesn't matter much what they use because, 'It's not the tool, it's the fool behind the tool'. It is important to have a decent set of clubs, but after that it's all developed talent: 98% individual, 2% equipment. You can't buy a game, you have to earn it.

There are many different ways to approach the game given that both physical and mental aspects are almost always involved. The less experienced a player is, the more physical the game is — for a beginner, it's 90% physical. There is a popular saying that 'golf is 90% mental'. If this is so, why do we have to practice all the physical stuff? This saying likely applies only to the expert player, yet ironically these are the game's best players and they practice the most! Their considerable investment of time and effort to building and fine-tuning physical skills would suggest a more intimate connection between skill competence and mental confidence — building confidence through consistency and consistency through confidence.

A regular practice routine will develop consistent muscle memory. Throughout these lessons we have been developing your knowledge base and your physical skills for golf. It's important to realize that these skills will be practiced over the long term, and improvement may be slow, but slow will be relative. How many balls are you willing to hit a week? If you hit 200 - 500 balls a week and play twice a week your improvement will be continuous. If you hit 50 balls once in a while and play semi-monthly, improvement will be minimal. Golf is a numbers game where regular practice is rewarded with results.

The purpose behind Smash & Carve is to provide you, the developing golfer, with the correct terminology, the key elements of movement, and a direct approach to learning and understanding the nuts and bolts of the golf swing. For now, you are able to communicate the language of the game and are armed with the understanding of contact and direction. Dedicating yourself today to a positive training program will help to encourage your steady progress as you continue to discover and enjoy the art of ball striking.

Amanda Minni

(Born Aug 1999)

Member of the Oregon State
Beavers Women's Golf Team
2017 - 2023 (DIV 1)

MBA degree 2023

Jace Minni

(Born Feb 2002)

Member of the Gonzaga Bulldogs
Men's Golf Team 2020 - 2024 (DIV 1)

Team Canada Junior Squad
Member in 2020

Business Administration Degree 2024

Scott Minni

A member of the PGA of Canada since 1985 and currently residing in Vancouver, BC, Canada, Scott is a 'Mentor' of the game! His 1996 Canadian Assistants title, 4 BCPGA titles (92,93,94,97) along with his 1999 BCPGA Teacher of the Year award, show that he has worthy credentials. Both of Scott's kids were on golf scholarships and played for Division 1 schools in the USA. Amanda played for Oregon State University (2017-2023) and Jace played for Gonzaga University in Spokane, Washington (2020-2024). The success of both Minni kids along with thousands of Scott's clients, show the long-term success of the Smash & Carve teaching method.

ONLINE LESSONS ARE AVAILABLE WITH SCOTT

$75 cad

scottminni99@gmail.com

www.smashandcarve.com

Steps to On-Line Lessons:

1. Make contact with Scott via email

2. Scott will instruct <u>WHEN</u> to send videos from both front and 'behind line' angles (5-10 seconds) with you explaining your game/issues in a short paragraph

3. Payment (etransfer) after Scott confirms receipt of your videos

4. Scott will give advice/guidance over email (1-2 paragraphs)

5. One follow-up question from client is welcome. Facetime or Zoom available on request

Meet Scott and watch an 8 minute Smash & Carve video lesson!

SCAN ME